Family & Business Constellations

CLAUDIO ALBERTO GONZÁLEZ

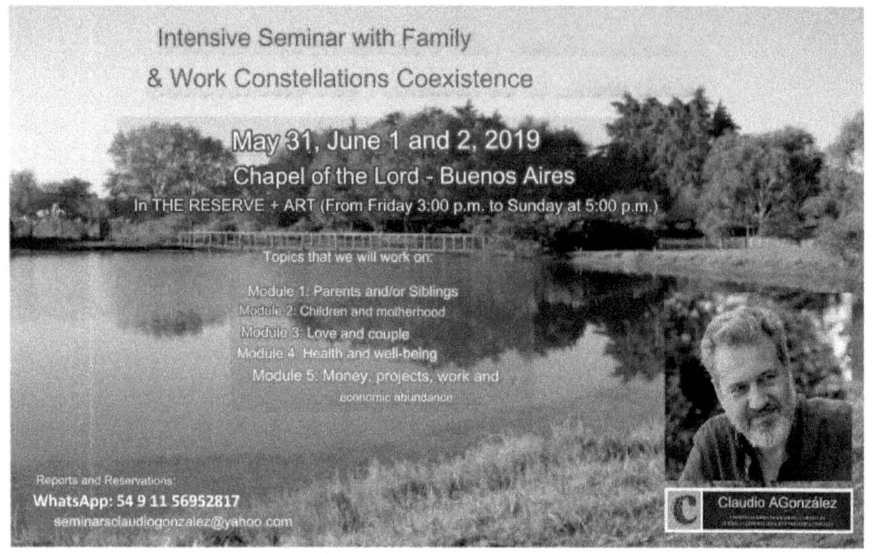

Copyright © 2019, 2023
Claudio Alberto González
All rights reserved

ISBN Paperback English 979-886-07679-7-3
ISBN Hardcover English 979-886-49140-5-2
First Edition in Spanish 978-108-73150-8-9

I

Version October 2023
v 48.104

Family & Business Constellations

Intensive Seminar with Coexistence

May 31 and June 1 and 2, 2019

The Reserve: Nature + Art

Capilla del Señor

Buenos Aires Argentina

CLAUDIO ALBERTO GONZÁLEZ

RAE Definitions

Constellation -Definition of RAE (Royal Spanish Academy 2019)

https://dle.rae.es/srv/search?&w=constelaci%C3%B3n

From lat. constellation, -ōnis.

1. f. A set of stars that, through imaginary strokes, form a drawing that evokes a specific figure.

2. f. Joint, harmonious meeting.

3. f. his. Climate or temper.

Family – Definition of RAE (Royal Spanish Academy – 2019)

https://dle.rae.es/srv/search?&w=familiar

From lat. familiaris.

1. adj. Belonging or relating to the family. A family custom.

2. adj. Previously known. 'His face is very familiar to me.'

3. adj. Said of the treatment: Plain and without ceremony.

4. adj. Said of a word, a phrase, language, style, etc.: Natural, simple and typical of normal and ordinary conversation.

5. adj. Said of the packaging of a commercial product: it is larger than normal and is generally cheaper.

6. adj. Said of a vehicle, especially a car: large capacity and with the rear luggage rack incorporated into the cabin.

7. adj. Said of a normal or pathological trait: that it is repeated within a family.

8.m. and f. Relative of a person.

9. m. Ecclesiastical or layman who accompanies or assists a bishop.

10. m. Servant of the community of a school.

11 m. Minister of the old ecclesiastical court of the Inquisition who was present at the arrests and other missions.

12. m. In the military order of Alcántara, a man who out of affection and devotion was admitted to it, offering free of charge, present or future, all or part of his property.

13. m. Person who took the insignia or habit of a religion, like the brothers of the third order.

14. m. Demon who was supposed to have dealings with a person he accompanied and served.

15 m. Person who has frequent and trusting contact with someone.

16. m. his. Domestic servant.

Labor – Definition of RAE (Royal Spanish Academy – 2019)

https://dle.rae.es/srv/search?&w=laboral

Of labor and -al.

1. adj. Belonging or relating to work, in its economic, legal and social aspect.

Claudio Alberto González

Experience and Track Record

https://linktr.ee/claudioalbertogonzalez

WhatsApp: +54(911) 5695-2817

Professional in the Marketing area with strategic thinking and a generalist vision of the business. He has more than 20 years of experience as a Manager, developed in National and International Direct Selling Companies, within the country and abroad. He is experienced in managing crisis situations and organizational change.

Since 2005 he has been dedicated to Consulting, Mentoring, Training, Internal Communication and Coaching. He has developed the Organizational Optimization Program ® (OOP) in which he also applies the Phenomenological approach, Systemic Interventions and Systemic Management in Organizations. His work is carried out in both the local and international markets (Argentina, Chile, México, Perú and Uruguay).

Since 2010 and until now, he has facilitated Workshops, Intensive Seminars, Individual Consultations and Consultations by videoconferences in family, work and organizational constellations in different Spaces and Theaters in Argentina and abroad. He also coordinates training groups and seminars in family, work and organizational constellations in Argentina, Chile, Uruguay, Perú and México, Spain and the United States. He leads "Transitando Etapas Vitales" Seminars that gave rise to his first book.

Diploma in Management Skills (PHD, University of Chile) 2004/2005. Postgraduate in Advanced Marketing (ISEAN Levy&Marketing) 1996/1997. Organizational Coach (LLC

Leading Learning Communities) 2001/2002. Bachelor's Degree in Marketing (Articulation at UCS Universidad Católica Salta) 1999/2000. Higher Technician in Marketing (FAECC Foundation for Higher Studies in Commercial Sciences) 1984/1988.

International Certification in Systemic Management and Organizational Constellations (UDEC, Universidad Multicultural Emilio Cárdenas of México. INFOSYON International Forum for System Constellations in Organizations and Talent Manager 2012/13). International Training in Organizational Constellations and Systemic Interventions (Center Bert Hellinger Argentina 2011). Family Constellations and Systemic Solutions (Bert Hellinger Argentina Center 2009/10). Personal and Organizational Enneagram (Argentine Enneagram Center 2001/03).

He has trained in intensive training with: Bert Hellinger (2010, 2014, 2015). Stephan Hausner (2009, 2014, 2016), Jan Jacob Stam (2011, 2012), Gunthard Weber (2011), Joan Garriga (2011), Claude Rosselet (2012), Siegfried Essen (2014), Mike Boxhall (2013), Tiiu Bolzmann (2009, 2010, 2011, 2012, 2013, 2014, 2015, 2016), Angélica Olivera de Malpica (2014, 2015), Cecilio Fernandez Regojo (2012, 20,13, 2014), María de los Hoyos (2009, 2010, 2011, 2012, 2013, 2014, 2015, 2016, 2017, 2018). Mayé Arredondo (2014).

Reached Advanced Level of Somatic Experiencing (Brazilian Trauma Association) (2016,2017,2018)

Author of the book *"Etapas Vitales"* published on Amazon Kindle (2019) with Ariel Castiglioni.

Between 2012 and 2014, he coordinated Systemic Coaching and Family Constellations workshops within the NGO "A Cielo Abierto", in Penitentiary Unit #40 in Buenos Aires, whose objective is to reduce violence among inmates, promote social reintegration and their work.

Foreword by a participant

(Who lived the workshop and the birth of this book)

Nine of us, who traveled from Concepción del Uruguay, arrived at Capilla del Señor. We were greeted by a wonderful paradisiacal place full of nature, large trees, various birds, a lake, an extensive meadow and autumn coloring the landscape.

I arrived very happy for having allowed myself to come, to have wanted to be here and to have been able to be here.

When I arrived, the entire group introduced ourselves and Claudio, humble and so friendly, greeted us and invited us to have a snack and then meet in the living room and begin the activities.

After introducing ourselves, he asked us what topics we were coming to work on or see. I really wasn't clear about what had brought me up or maybe I was scared to touch on the topic that bothers me the most in my life, since it is my big secret, and I didn't know if I wanted to say it. Maybe for fear of knowing and losing that love or for fear of being judged. Luckily, I was not the first to speak and as the other participants shared their topics, I became clearer.

After having gone through and explained my topic, it occurred to me to write:

> *"It's like a kind of confessional, deciding the issue, becoming aware, recognizing where you are, your pain, your thoughts, your emotions.*
>
> *Your shame goes away, you tell it, you lose the fear of being judged, and you free yourself, you accept yourself, just as you are at this moment.*
>
> *You take charge, responsible for your decisions; you open the door to change, to walk towards the life you dream of."*

After almost three days together, seeing and participating in approximately twenty Constellations, sharing empowerment dynamics, ordering priorities, changing life paradigms towards confidence that I can be and do what makes me happy, I am leaving with the strength to act towards reaching my desires, to risk myself for what I want, without fear of what they will say, with the strength and support of my family and with the necessary information to make decisions for growth, to be more myself, free and naive in love.

I thank Claudio for this meeting, for offering himself so openly and sharing his experience and knowledge.

I thank the place, the nature that contained us, the wonderful people who took care of us, and the warmth of the group that allowed me to learn more and heal.

Thank you.

Anonymous
6/2/2019
Capilla del Señor
Buenos Aires

Introduction by Claudio Alberto González

This is my first book about Constellations that for years I have dreamed of writing. Although there is a lot of material on this topic, I am happy that you have chosen to read this book, it contains my essence.

I have been preparing for this for 57 years with the great luck of having been able to count on great and wise teachers of life that I honor today.

In this book I tell you that it is possible to reinvent yourself by giving yourself ideas for it. You will be able to experience and feel present in one of my Constellation Seminars, which are all unique and unrepeatable. You will be able to get excited, laugh, think and dream. It can even take you to action... and that would be the greatest gift for me, because that's why I wrote it, for you, to help you and assist you on your flight.

While I was writing it, I remembered something from my story, I remembered constellations that impacted me, that I carry in my heart and that I now choose to tell you.

I wrote it in a simple, enjoyable, easy-to-read way and with many of my own examples. And I also include material that I use to empower others and myself. So that you can better organize yourself and make it easier for you to achieve your dreams!

I want to dedicate this book to Life and the Future, to my beloved children Joaquín and Abril who are wonderful, to their mother Teresa to whom I was married for twenty years. I dedicate it to Fede and Nico, my two oldest unborn children. To my parents Neli and Alberto, to my grandparents Conce, Coca, Félix and Valerio, to my brothers Marce, Gaby and Maxi, my sisters-in-law Marianela and Vero, to my nieces and nephews Facundo, Agustina, Nicolas, Catarina, Sofía, Felipe, Federico and those who will come! To my friends of soul and iron! All of them are a very important part of my life, they are my family system of origin and my current family system.

I leave for last the wonderful people who accompanied me this weekend and without them it would have been impossible to write this book. Many of us have known each other for a long time, and I feel very happy that they have participated with so much love and put their best effort into it. Thank you thank you thank you, Andrea, Araceli, Claudia, Cristina, Débora, Gabriela, Gastón, Gisela, Griselda, Hernán, Laura, María Rosa, Mirta, Neli, Nely, Raquel, Susana and Virginia, thank you thank you thank you for so much!!!

Let's get started!

What are Systemic Constellations?

All of us are crossed by multiple systems:

- a family system of origin (where we come from),
- a current family system (the one we make up with our partner and children),
- a labor system, and
- an organizational system.

Our body is also a system. That is to say, where a system exists, with this wonderful tool called Systemic Constellations, we can work to organize it.

What normally happens is that when we have difficulties in some area, they are reflected in others, we repeat many stories, and also many tragedies. What is not resolved on one level or ancestral plane passes to the next, and this is how we come carrying chains of invisible loyalties that out of love we sustain and out of loyalty we repeat, causing a lot of pain.

Depending on the area where we operate, the constellations are called:

- Constellations of our family of origin.
- Constellations of our current family.
- Constellations in the field of health.
- Business constellations and organizational constellations.

The Constellation is a systemic and phenomenological tool; it is systemic because it responds within any type of system, and it is phenomenological because we are impartial observers of the movement and evolution of the phenomena that manifest when performing it. It is very versatile, and it allows you to observe the organization that the members have within their system.

All of us believe that we occupy an indisputable role; we are children of, spouse of, mother/father of. The interesting thing arises when, upon starting a Constellation, we discover that nothing is what it seems, that out of love and loyalty to my parents I am supporting them as if they were my own children/grandparents, abandoning or not being able to have enough strength to make my own life and projects happen.

It is a methodology that we use to analyze all the components of a person and their environment from a systemic point of view, that is, as a "whole" system.

The person who brought Family Constellations to light was Bert Hellinger, born in Germany on December 16, 1925. Bert Hellinger is a German philosopher, theologian and pedagogue and currently, at 94 years old, he continues to give conferences and seminars about Family Constellations in different places around the world.

He discovered that there are orders and laws that govern systems, that when a system is disordered, it causes unhappiness to its members. In this way, the systemic ordering that causes a Constellation allows Order to provoke and enable the harmonious flow of Love.

After Bert Hellinger's Family Constellations, Gunthard Weber continued developing the topic of Constellations and from his studies came Organizational Constellations and systemic management (which I currently carry out in the organizations and companies that hire me to analyze organization charts and processes).

Thanks to the great teacher Tiiu Bolzmann, who brought the knowledge to Argentina when she settled here in 1998, and then to Bert Hellinger himself, today Family Constellations have expanded as a practice throughout the American continent.

We define this process as a series of steps:

• **Identify** the particularities of a person.

• **Sort them** in an image.

• **Transfer them** to a set of people or objects.

• **Intervene** to integrate, include and thank.

One of the definitions of the word ***"Intervene"*** is "temporarily taking someone else's property," and that is exactly what I do in this process.

When I perform a Constellation on a person, I take for a few moments into my heart and mind the properties that I see, observe and feel. This is how I connect, vibrating with her feelings in accordance with her. Once the connection between my own system and the system provided by the constellated person has been achieved, the system tells us where the solution is oriented, it shows us where the path is. Many times, the solution is where the person cannot see or where it hurts the most to see. That is where the system shows us the way, so that by connecting with what the person cannot see, with what is excluded or forgotten, a door of access to healing and liberation opens. Deep pain and emotion will possibly well up with tears from within. They are tears that purify her, giving her ancestors their liberation and giving her the pride of having been brave and having had the courage to get there. The gift (the present) is the love that begins to flow in all its forms, with sounds, smells and colors. Then the person is free, with clarity, relief and gratitude. That person is no longer alone, now her father and mother are behind her, and her ancestors also support her. Together they will take care of her, love her, protect her and encourage her to achieve her dreams with them, which are also theirs, since now the integrated person is also them and they all live in her.

Performing a Constellation is assisting the person to integrate their life, their stories, their past, their present and their future. Integrate and include is the goal, taking as its axis the specific request that the person requests. This will allow the person to be excited, integrated and incorporate what they want, as well as their heart opening to compassion and acceptance of how things are. It is surrendering to their own system with love, understanding that it will be the one who, in its compassionate mantle, will heal it.

Up to this point we have paved the way. We have worked on understanding our experience and asking ourselves questions about our purpose. We finish the paved stage by talking about the moment, the question **When.**

In a Constellations exercise we can use elements to compose a system (people in a room, chess pieces on a board, dolls or other chosen objects).

This system has a process that changes until the organization that best represents us is found. At first, we may feel it in disharmony, moving the elements without fully understanding how to represent our interior. Here a duly trained facilitator stimulates with questions the creation of a new system (new drawing or formation of elements) so that the set of elements comes into harmony.

To achieve this harmony, the facilitator may ask people, or the constellated person, to say certain healing phrases, or to do certain actions such as thanking, hugging or removing a component from the system.

My intention in this book is to introduce you to the components of the Constellation so that you obtain tools that will help you order the elements of your lives.

Currently there are a large number of books that talk about Family Constellations from different approaches. If you are interested in getting started or deepening this knowledge, I suggest two books that will help you in this purpose: *"The spring does not have to ask for the way"* by Bert Hellinger Editorial *Alma* Lepik, and *"What are Family Constellations?"* by Tiiu Bolzmann Editorial *Alma* Lepik.

Extracted from my book *"Vital Stages"* published on Amazon Kindle (2019) that we wrote with my friend Ariel Castiglioni and that I now allow myself to share with you.

The Orders of Love

Although, as I said previously, there are many books that talk about the Orders of Love, in these lines I will seek to detail the topic.

Bert Hellinger discovered that there are orders and laws that govern systems. There are two types, the Orders of Love at the level of Personal Consciousness, and the Orders of Love at the level of Family Consciousness.

Consciousness or Personal Soul

The Consciousness or Personal *Soul* is at a conscious level and defines the laws of coexistence with respect to:

1. The Links.
2. The Balance between Giving and Taking.
3. The Rules and Values.

Links

From the moment we are born we are linked to a system of origin and when we develop, we shape our current system. We maintain this connection beyond our lives.

Although we no longer have relationships with people, the bond is indissoluble.

For example, we are linked to our great-great-grandparents, even though we have never met them, and therefore we have never related.

Another example would be after a divorce, even if the relationship no longer existed, the bond persists.

The strongest bond is with our parents, siblings and grandparents within the system of origin and with our partners, children and friends in our current system.

Balance between Giving and Taking

In life inside and outside the family there is a permanent exchange, giving and receiving as they normally say. The difference between Taking and Receiving is that Taking is active and generates commitment, while Receiving is passive. It would be the equivalent between Living/Subsisting (Receiving) and Honoring Life (Taking).

For relationships to last over time, it is necessary that this balance between Giving and Taking is maintained. We can see many examples in couples where one Gives more and the other Takes more. If this Give and Take is not balanced, it will not be sustained over time.

This type of imbalance can also occur when there are difficulties between partners, peers or siblings. The only case in which it cannot be balanced is in the relationship between Parents and Children. Since parents Give life and children Take life. The only way to balance is by giving life or doing service to others.

The Rules and Values

It would be equivalent to the implicit or explicit code of coexistence that governs each family, founded on the values of the family system.

It can range from the time the television is turned off, eating with the in-laws every Sunday, and countless traditions based on rules. From a rule, the most explicit, to only having permission to interact with people who share the same religion, the most implicit.

Consciousness or Family Systemic Soul

The Family Systemic Consciousness or *Soul* is at an unconscious level and seeks to include all members of the System and its laws are:

- Of Belonging.
- Make room for those who were excluded in their time.
- The Hierarchies.

Law of Belonging

We all have the right to belong to our Family system, even despite what we have done in the course of our lives that was not approved by our family. Here, there is no distinction between good and bad, the important thing is that it belongs to the system. Among them are previous partners, deceased children, very dear family members who, due to the pain that their absence causes, no one else talks about them, excluding them. Also, the unborn, which I group into four types, induced abortions, spontaneous abortions, those that the woman did not register and only took as a loss. And the fourth that is not considered are abortions resulting from fertility treatments that failed to prosper.

Make room for those who were excluded in their time

The Consciousness or Family Systemic *Soul* seeks to include all of the above since for it they are the most important thing.

They are important because without them we would never have been born. The way it chooses to include the excluded is to randomly involve a newborn with that soul. We may be involved by more than one soul from our own Family System. The way in which we realize the existence of the implications is when in the course of our lives we encounter difficulties, health problems, situations that are repeated or obstacles to moving forward.

A Systemic Constellation allows us to make such an implication explicit, giving its place to the soul that involved us. Thus, each one is freed, in the case of our ancestors to rest in peace and in our case to continue life much lighter.

The Hierarchies

There is an order and for Family Consciousness, the one who entered the System before has priority over the one who did it later. What cannot be healed on an ancestral plane continues to the next. We may be carrying, out of love for our ancestors, chains of invisible loyalties in which we repeat stories, since we may be affected by up to nine generations. This is how women often present to the consultation afflicted with loneliness within a couple, repeating stories from their mother, grandmother and perhaps much further back. Something similar happens with men in whom economic abundance eludes them, repeating ancestral stories.

The constellations were in my destiny

First, I would like to tell you a little about how I became involved in the world of systemic constellations.

It was a long road, the one that every seeker begins to travel without knowing where it will take them.

Since I was a child, I had the great luck of enjoying my four grandparents, who were very loving, different and complementary. I had the great joy of integrating different perspectives and experiences through them. I loved listening to them, and my curiosity was feasted on their stories and experiences. From the sweetness and pampering of my grandmothers Coca and Conce who crawled with me under the dining room table, to the teachings of my grandparents Félix, a wise scholar living inside an honest accountant, and Valerio, charismatic and innate entrepreneur who as a child lived through the poverty in Spain and together with his father Servando, they arrived in Argentina to become an important metallurgical businessman.

Since I was a child, I knew that my challenge was to find the balance between these examples that life gave me. Being able to think and integrate the various combinations, such as wisdom with money and business, wealth and success associated with good, honesty and integrity, that abundance is combined with desert, that Giving is in balance with Receiving, that love joins the vocation and the family...that the family coexists in peace and harmony. Learn to discern between my dreams and fantasies. How to enter the real world without it being at the expense of my dreams. Transitioning towards my dreams with fear, but as part of the learning necessary to achieve my successes. Hold failures with dignity and compassion for myself as I continue to learn. Learn to take care of myself and love myself more, because, if I don't, then I can't do it with others.

Knowing the risk and adrenaline that is felt when being able to navigate the ledge between limiting models and challenging dreams. Live life as an adventure in which nothing is yet written, that on the turn of the page or perhaps tomorrow I will find what I have been looking for so much. Search…that is a word that brings me to treasure hunters and is very related to chance. Don't you think it's time for us to change searching to FIND since he who seeks does not always find, but he who goes out to find...FINDS.

After having gone through the model of having to be a good son, student, etc., to the personal satisfaction of my parents and grandparents, I discovered, for example, that engineering was not for me, and life led me to find marketing, which I was passionate about. Due to an error of interpretation, added to my ignorance and the bad press that sales had in my family, all my life I refused to practice it, the same thing happened to me with the idea of working in a dependency relationship.

This is how I developed my entrepreneurial spirit by doing a little bit of everything, in the image and likeness of my father Alberto and grandfather Valerio, while still being counterbalanced by the fear and caution of my scholarly grandfather Félix.

All my life I refused to sell until life and my needs led me to encounter my own fears, which were about selling, rejection, and working in a dependency relationship.

I discovered then that the first thing was to identify my fears and that my exit and evolution passed through there, the exit, like an energetic vortex, was to go through my own fears.

I discovered that I was good at listening to people, and that my words gained strength and power from understanding, from active listening oriented to the solution, to assist, by helping others with their problems.

Life gave me the gift of being able to experiment and make mistakes many times, to melt down literally and financially twice, to have gone from having several businesses to having to start from scratch again, to work non-stop, to persevere and get up once again after each fall.

I also refused, out of family loyalty, to work in a dependent relationship, but life is relentless and knows how to make us kneel, so we have to learn. So, one day I found myself looking very angry at the sky saying… What do you want from me?? What am I not realizing and what do I need to learn?? Inside me was the answer, this arrogance and haughtiness that years later I understood would find its way by starting to work in a dependent relationship and in sales. Learning to lower your head and obey. It was starting over, but this time in something I truly feared and in which I was totally vulnerable. This time I had to ASK for help with sincere humility.

From my thirties until almost my fifties, I dedicated myself to working in employee relationships and in sales.

In less than ten years, a fearful and insecure sales apprentice went from selling car pre-saving plans on the street (a promise to purchase zero km cars in 84 installments) to the general management of the company SwissJust in Chile and director of the Andean regional leading to Chile, Perú and Ecuador. Having passed through the commercial management of the Company in Argentina.

Over time, thanks to the jobs and roles I played, I realized that I was always dedicated to selling. I liked to listen to people and in that listening I understood what the person needed emotionally. And I was able to transfer the satisfaction of that emotional need to the product I was selling, whatever it was. That is why I was able to unite and relate needs and show that there was always a plan B, that we could find together a different way out, a third position.

There I understood that the key was to listen to others and provide a solution to their problem and need, not a mere product. My office has always been little more than an office, where all the people from any area or sector came to talk about some problem. This was my great school of active listening.

I owe my adult professional career to three companies, all related to the world of beauty and health.

As I write these lines, I have just discovered that I have always been interested in people feeling good and comfortable with themselves by looking good in the mirror. This is how my path began, within the world of cosmetic companies, so that people could see themselves more beautiful and from there improve their self-esteem (which was still external) and today through my Family Constellations Seminars and Labor, I work so that they can see themselves beautiful and at peace with themselves, with their own soul and ancestors.

Thanks to Framesi International (Italian hair cosmetics company) I discovered and developed my sales and negotiation skills.

Thanks to Jafra Cosmetics International (American direct sales cosmetics company) I discovered and developed my management and leadership skills. In which my great teachers of ethics, professionalism, management and understanding of the direct selling business were them: Carmen de Errasti and Alfredo Solé.

Thanks to SwissJust Argentina, Chile, Perú, Uruguay, México and America (Swiss direct sales company for health and well-being) I discovered and developed my personal expertise in directing, passion, mysticism and teamwork. Thanks to the vision and passion of Sam Mizrahi who gave rise to the mystical G4: Juan Manuel Freire, Eduardo Fernandez, Alejandro Maure and who is speaking to you. A high-performance team that was formed in Argentina in 2000 transformed the Company and all its subsidiaries in America. So many good moments, so many hours and dreams shared, this was so great that it deserves another book (which I am working on).

I discovered that I could motivate, excite, make others vibrate and passionate so that they could make their dreams come true, so that thousands of women could find and develop their forgotten skills. That many of them, hurt by the hits of life, entered the company like shy Cinderellas, believed in my commitment to them and transformed in a short time into great successful businesswomen. Remembering each one of them going up on stage to receive flowers, awards and applause really moves me. It was our great triumph and my great gift. It's like I once said in one of those scenarios...

seeing them so radiant and happy is as if I could see my own mother in that recognition. That because of love, submission and fear could not expand her own potential.

Today with my work I seek to bring physical, mental and emotional well-being to the world, transcending companies, ideologies and borders. Wherever I am required, there I will be letting myself flow in time and space, led by the vocation and happiness that vibrating on this path of assistance to others, and to you, causes me.

Thank you for being on the other side as you give me a reason to keep moving forward. I found the tool that I looked for so many years and that allows me to be there to assist, to accompany, to listen and thus be able to heal us.

How did my two worlds integrate today?

My position as manager and director in the companies in which I intervened transformed me into a results-oriented leader. In other words, my success was based on the results of my words. If my words failed to generate actions in my teams, the result was not achieved for me. The success of these people was my success.

In that process I discovered something magical. The achievements of these people were closely linked to their emotional states. And without realizing it I began to work with them on their personal issues, to help them find solutions where they only saw problems, to see things that their unresolved personal issues or their anger did not allow them to develop their virtues to the fullest. So, I began to delve into their personal lives with questions, showing them another perspective, suggesting seeing topics that could be in some way related to those attitudes that were cutting their wings, and in that way, I managed to enter their hearts and help them heal and fly. That made their work results grow remarkably.

At that moment I learned my first important lesson. I had found, not my job, but my vocation. My vocation was to unshackle people from their ties, their mental shackles, their unresolved grief, their broken ties, their disconnection from their loved ones, their poorly healed wounds; so that they not only worked better but also lived better. I realized that this, which was genuinely coming out of me, transcended me and my own benefit. I did it because I was passionate, excited and because it fed my soul to see people, after these interventions, feel relief, hope and encourage them to make their dreams come true.

That was my first realization that my path was along the path of helping to heal. Without planning it I became a motivational trainer bringing well-being wherever I went and generating results for others.

One day, without even knowing what they were or what they were for, I found this passion for Systemic Constellations. It's much more accurate to say that the Constellations found me. Without thinking about it I signed up to train as a constellator, I didn't know much about them, I just knew that, if I could reconcile with my past, I would be able to move towards a better and happier future. And that's how the signs on the road started telling me "Your path is this way."

The Constellations reconciled me with my father

In my first constellator training class, I had to do an exercise of honoring parents. That was my unexpected and best gift, since I had been estranged from my father for more than two years. I remember that my father was angry, he wouldn't talk to me, and he wouldn't let me get close to him. After the exercise, a mantle of compassion and understanding lowered over me and gave me the courage and humility to reach out. The next day was my birthday and I decided to call him on the phone, I told him three words that I later learned were magical within the constellations.

- ✓ **1. YES** 'Hello dad, I'm Claudio.' (I recognize you as the great one). 'Happy birthday,' Dad told me.
- ✓ **2. THANK YOU** 'For giving me life.'
- ✓ **3. PLEASE** 'Tomorrow I celebrate my birthday and if you want, I would very much like to invite you to my house.'

And he came. And right there, without preambles, without blaming or recriminations, our reconciliation process began.

Six months later my father died. And every day I wonder if I had not done what I did thanks to the constellations, I would never have been able to reconcile with him. Today I know that if he had not done it and he had died, my grieving process would have been much more complicated and traumatic.

Thanks to the fact that I often comment on my story of reconciliation with dad, several people have come so that I could assist them in their reunion, which makes me very happy for them. I hope that these lines can help many more people, since being distanced from our parents is something that takes away a lot of peace from us.

Why, for what and for whom I wrote this book

Writing a book about the experiences I face day after day as a constellator is a dream come true. I have been making thousands of constellations for years and in each experience, I feel like the first time. Seeing how, through my questions and new approaches, a person who is suffering, can see what they could not, understand what they refused, feel their body and posture empower them and finally the tears. When the tears fall, the heart opens. That openness, that relief, is a gift to me.

A constellator is not a guru, he is not a preacher, nor a shaman. A constellator is a channel, he is a facilitator, who manages, with his interventions, his questions, his reading of the position, his reading between the lines, to get to the bottom of the issues, even when the person being constellated is focused on another aspect of their life.

A constellator is a person who has consciously or unconsciously lived his life in the service of humanity, who over time added knowledge, experiences and skills, capitalizing and enhancing it to serve, in which he ends up connecting his own system to the patient's system, and that through love he can facilitate and channel the gift of assistance through the Being.

That is my passion, to help heal lives, people, families, couples. It took me a while and a few turns in the revolving door to understand it. But once I stopped at this station, I could feel the world stop spinning and inner peace invaded me, mixed with an inexhaustible energy eager to understand and do more.

This between you and me

How would you like your ideal life? Have you ever stopped to think? To dream? Imagine yourself in a nature reserve, fresh and pure air around you, in contact with nature, walking in silence, and traveling through your depth, to finally expand. This always happens after working on the dynamics and exercises that I offer in my seminars. I have worked on these same exercises and dynamics for many years, with thousands of people, and in several countries, always faithful to my style: very seriously, very professional and above all very down to earth.

I hope that, as a reader of this book, you also get on this train that is already underway. I only ask that you trust me. Not only will I take care of you, but I assure you that I will help you.

This book could be your opportunity for change. Read it, enjoy it and join the change. I'm waiting for you.

Memories of constellations that gave meaning to my vocation

I want to share with you some constellations that, depending on the case and context, I share in my talks. Some of these and other constellations remain in the depths of my heart, giving meaning to my work. Some that to this day I haven't mentioned because I am waiting for the feedback of their resolution.

Couple waiting for a home

In 2018, in a constellation I did in a theater, I remember a young couple that had a girl. They decided to come to constellation because they couldn't be granted housing under a social plan; they had already been waiting for two years.

It didn't take me long to discover the problem: there was no communication between him and his father. He refused to reconcile with his father, his criteria and generational differences kept them apart.

'The house is waiting for you, it needs you to reconcile with your father,' I told him. 'The time it takes you to reconcile with your father is how long it will take for the house to arrive to you.' I interrupted the constellation so that the healing could be carried out by the true protagonists (a son with his father). I also remember that the young man was upset with me, waiting for the constellation to conclude with the happy ending that he expected. But it was not like that, since 'I am at the service of the Family System,' I told him, 'And I cannot force things, you need to open your heart to your father and until you do this, your issue will not be resolved." When people are not prepared or lack the ability to open their hearts, only time and some tasks that we propose will facilitate this process.

Days later I found out that the next day the young man went to his father's house and stayed with him for two days talking and settling their affairs. Four days later he was given the house.

Some people come looking for solutions, expecting the constellation and the constellator to solve what they are not willing to do. My function is to indicate the best way for the family or work system to be organized according to systemic principles. Most of the time the ordering can occur within the framework of the constellation, sometimes it requires more time, it requires that a mantle of compassion flows towards the *Querent* so that their heart opens to internal and external reconciliation. As I said above, I am at the service of the System that is much bigger than us. If the System starts to be organized, the members will be increasingly happy.

Fibromyalgia and Depression

This story belongs to a lady of the ninth Septennium (56 to 63 years old, we will explain the septens later) who suffered from fibromyalgia. She was heavily medicated and still unable to work. Her hands were numb and powerless. She had worked in gastronomy all her life, but her current situation prevented it. She loved what she did, but she was very distraught and discouraged. One day she makes up her mind and contacts me to constellate on that topic.

She tells me that her first grandson was born with a tumor in his arm, and it had to be amputated. After 3 months of intensive care the child died.

Her daughter, the boy's mother, went into a great depression so she had to take care of everything, including her 9-year-old granddaughter.

We constellated by working on the baby's farewell and her grief, so she could close it in a healthy way.

Shortly after I received her call. She was another woman. Her energy gushed like spring water and her voice had rejuvenated. She told me that after the constellation, fifteen days later she went back to work as if nothing had happened.

The following month her daughter came to see me, the baby's mother was still in a deep depressive state and had no desire to live.

In the constellation she laid on the floor, hugging his son and wanting to go with him too. I remember that it was a very difficult situation for me as a constellator, since I was seeing how a mother wanted to let herself die, following her little son. I remember it as if it were today, it was around 5:00 p.m. on a beautiful afternoon in Tigre, Buenos Aires. In the constellation and as representatives there was the representative of the child curled up by the mother (the *Consultant*), lying on the floor. A little further back was the representative of her 9-year-old daughter who was being accompanied by the representative of her father.

At that moment and faced with this heartbreaking scene that I was seeing, where all the people in the workshop could not contain their tears, I remember that internally I declared myself incompetent, asking SOMETHING BIGGER, without knowing who, how would I be able to cope with such a tragedy...

And I began to tell the mother that there is a movement called "I follow you," in which one soul out of love follows the other, that there are times when people get sick or have accidents following that loved one. I also told her that if she wanted, she could choose to follow her son and die... but there is an additional risk and that is that your 9-year-old daughter's soul, faced with such pain, will also decide to follow you and die with you.

When the mother heard me say these words…she looked at me, she looked at her son, at her daughter and with hatred she shouted "NO, NOT her," she kissed her son on the forehead, left him lying on the floor and when she started to get up to go to hug her daughter, at that precise moment, a rooster crowed twice, breaking total silence. Her mother sat up crying and hugged her daughter to whom she clung for a long time. After that moment I told the mother: "the fact that a rooster crowed in this place twice was the signal for you to get up and see that you were doing the right thing." I will never forget that experience.

Shortly after, the mother came out of the depressive state she was in, six months later she returned to work, found a partner again, and about a year and a half later she was a mother again.

Cancer

Once a lady from Neuquén came to make her constellation. The issue she brought to constellate was that she had been suffering the terminal phase of cancer for about two years.

I remember asking her:

'What happened two years ago?'

She looked up and with tears told me that she had murdered her husband. That she was not imprisoned by the terminal state of her illness. When I began to constellate, I saw that she loved him deeply and that, in a fit of passionate jealousy, she had been blinded and killed him. She came from a matriarchal family. There was no place for men there. None of the women in that family had a man next to her and, in her case, there was no permission to have one either. This is an example of how invisible chains of loyalty to our ancestors sometimes work.

During the constellation she managed to say goodbye to him with love, she really loved him. It was a very heartfelt and emotional farewell.

After the constellation she was very relieved and I mentioned to her that, although the death penalty does not exist in our country, she had inflicted it on herself. After six months, the lady died peacefully, feeling forgiven and certain that he had forgiven her too.

She left this world with the full conviction of finding him again in another life and thus resuming her love eternally.

Love of motherhood

A little over a year ago I was contacted by a young 38-year-old woman who, even after repeatedly seeking motherhood, was not able to achieve it. The obstacle was related to the pride and arrogance that this woman had and that she felt towards her own mother. Something very unique happened to her in this constellation and it was that when she arrived, she was emotionally collapsed and desperate because of the feeling that her possibility of being a *mother* was dissipating, her partner was distancing from her and that everything she had fought for was fading away. It was a constellation that touched my soul. As representatives I put the *Consultant*, her mother, and in a hidden way, the motherhood that was distant. At that time the *Consultant* was looking at her mother's representative, she knelt down, clung to her mother's feet and with a heartbreaking cry, she asked, begged, "Mom, please help me, I need you...I can't take it anymore," at that moment the mother bent down, hugging her daughter with her whole body and snuggled her. A few seconds later, the representative of motherhood approaches her and hugs them both. The final image of the constellation was now sculpted by Mother, Daughter and Motherhood fused into a single sphere. A year later another baby was crawling around the world.

How the pain of an abandoned mother conditions the future of her son

A couple of years ago, on one of my trips, a mother came to the consultation with her two children, a daughter in her twenties and a teenage son. The three of them sat in front of me, the mother in the middle of her children, "what family issue are you coming for?" I asked them. "Do all three of you have the same problem?" they look at each other, they answer no. "We come in a bunch because there are no secrets between us, and my children will be the ones that are going to constellate," the mother says. "Do you want to constellate?" I laugh and ask the daughter and son "And do you prefer it to be in front of your mother or in private?." "In private!" they answered me.

"Ok," I told everyone, "So which one of you do I start with? I'll appreciate it if the rest stay in the waiting room." The simple memory of their mother's face (humorless) never fails to make me laugh.

That's how I first constellated the daughter about a matter of love disagreements, and after a few months she found a good love. For the second turn, the 17-year-old boy remains, with whom we constellate about a topic related to his vocation as an artist and singer, which conflicted with his mother's wishes for him of becoming an engineer. During the constellation process, it emerges that he did not know his biological father since, according to his mother, it was not necessary. In conclusion: we constellated, and the *Consultant* left vigorous to take the strength of his biological father, added to the deep desire to know him.

This is part of the story; the interesting thing was what happened the next day when at nine in the morning I received the following WhatsApp message from the boy's mother:

Mother's WhatsApp: "I find it hard to believe that a therapist would tell a 17-year-old child to look for his biological father. Isn't this what the Constellations tool is supposed to do? If a subject in your system is not available, for whatever reason, the tool with healing phrases repairs the absence and the system is ordered. You don't need to physically look for it. The only thing you will achieve is that he will be rejected again by someone who does not even deserve to be called a biological father. I am extremely complicated with this issue, Claudio."

After reading the message several times and feeling the pain of that mother, with all my love I respond:

"Hello, how are you? I understand you; the constellations are at the service of reconciliation and integration. That's why I made your son record the Constellation, so that you can hear it too. We are all children of a father and a mother, luckily he has a father from the heart who loves and supports him, but it is not enough to give him the strength he needs to face the problems he has to work on. Sooner or later, this was going to manifest itself and it is much better for this topic to appear now to prevent it from adding to frustrations as a couple, self-esteem, personal value and professional vocation, in addition to work (areas that fall within the ancestral strength of the biological father). What I propose is that you include that man in your heart, the father that you chose (consciously or unconsciously) for him to be his father. Just including it in your heart will allow your child to feel more whole and stronger. When one parent rejects the other, they unintentionally reject the 50% that lives inside their own child. I find that your son is a wonderful and very mature man who speaks very well of you, who raised him, but there are internal aspects that have him restless and in the initial image of the Constellation, you could see that who was appearing in his own future (and also in yours) and that you both looked at, was his biological father. Once again, I suggest that your openness to being able to forgive, let go and include his father in your heart will be of great help so that everything can be ordered harmoniously for everyone. I send you a big hug."

Mom's WhatsApp:

"Thank you, next time, I will constellate with you. I absolutely believe in the greater good and if you appeared in our lives, it is to be an agent of growth and healing, that's how I see it. I never took it upon myself to work much on the topic with my son, since many channelings told me that it was not a topic. His soul chose to arrive that way. Do not doubt that I will do everything humanly possible to help my son and heal this part of me, which woke up on Saturday, which I thought was resolved, but I found myself in a lot of pain and anger due to the abandonment. See you and thank you. We are onions, each layer does its own thing."

A couple of months later, she returned to the same city, the mother attended an Intensive Constellations Seminar, to continue working on herself. There she tells me that as a result of the constellation of her son, she told him about his father and paved the way for them to get to know each other. Her son made the decision to follow his vocation and study acting as well as singing. Now she is very happy!

Six months later this mother committed to her children demonstrated it again and this time she and her two children took a new Intensive Seminar, which was truly wonderful and very healing for the entire family system, for the three of them and for their children's fathers.

Objective of the seminar

The main objective of this seminar was, as in all my meetings, to heal, free and empower ourselves. In these meetings you can really heal and unblock those things that prevent you from getting where you want because we work on all important areas of life.

If you are needing it, read this book and attend my next seminar. Find the one that best suits your possibilities and come. Check cities and days worldwide on https://linktr.ee/claudioalbertogonzalez or on my WhatsApp +54 (911) 5695-2817.

I'll wait for you!!!

Seminar dynamics

This seminar that gave rise to this book took place from Friday, May 31, at 3 pm, until Sunday, June 2, 2019, at 6 pm. The coexistence was structured in modules of 4/5 hours each, with a total of 5 modules. In each module the following topics were worked on:

- Parents and/or Siblings.
- Children and Motherhood.
- Love and Couple.
- Health and Wellbeing.
- Money, projects, jobs and economic abundance.

Links with Parents

The issues that we have not resolved with our parents, whether or not they are on this earth, is advisable that we consider very seriously closing them. As long as we keep issues unresolved and unclosed, they keep our gaze anchored in the past, in what already was, in death, preventing us from focusing on the present and future. That starts from the acceptance of "what is." This means that, beyond what your parents gave you, they will no longer be able to give you. We demand and expect our parents to be exemplary, considerate, healthy, sane, upright, coherent and super powerful, while we, their children, have the reputation of being imperfect, fearful and insecure. And now we as adults ask ourselves... what do our children want and expect from me???

In the seminar we work so that everyone can close this stage to start something new and understand that now it depends exclusively on each one of us. This way we will be able to gain the strength we need to move forward fully.

Relationships with brothers or sisters.

The relationship we have with our siblings reflects our childhood; the rivalries caused by showing ourselves to our parents to be loved by them. That sparkle in our eyes when mom or dad gifted us something, or congratulated us, or hugged us. The competition between siblings for that love, for that part of love. We are all children of that love that sometimes manifests itself in painful ways. There are times when today's arguments or differences are the old disputes over the tricycle or the ball. Other times selfishness is nothing more than the desire not to share parents.

I have been consulted many times about inheritances that are blocked and do not flow to the children, and the constellation has clearly shown us that perhaps it is because one of the children was angry with one of their parents or cannot accept that they have died. Accepting the inheritance would be recognizing that the parents are no longer here or recognizing that the father was right.

How long has it been since you spoke to your sibling? How long has it been since you hugged them? These links are very important for the balance of our emotional system. We must cleanse them, heal them and honor them because only then will we have peace. Our siblings are a very important part of our system of origin and healing our bond with them is improving our relationships with our peers (coworkers, neighbors, partners, colleagues, partners, ex-partners).

Love and couple

If love is a little indifferent to you, or either comes and goes, or maybe what should have happened didn't. Are you sure that you closed something that was not completely resolved in a past relationship? Were you able to say goodbye to that love, did you close the duel? Since, if we did not close the love duel, it is very likely that we will repeat the stories and attract people with the same undesirable characteristics that we attracted, or that we will go for the opposite (which is not good either), or even that we will be left alone.

In this seminar we will be able to generate new and healthy spaces, free of wounds and leave the emotional space free to receive good love, which, if we are available, will be waiting for us.

Duels

To heal from grief, you have to go through a process. If the process is not carried out correctly, we are left with unresolved duels. From mom, from dad, from a brother, from a friend, from a partner. Life is about the future, about projects, about what is coming. If we do not resolve these duels, unfortunately, we can remain trapped in the past, or in grief eternally without achieving emotional freedom. Here together we manage to let go of the past and complete the duels in order to move through the present and the future in peace.

Maternity

Motherhood can sometimes be elusive or be a project that for some reason cannot be realized. In this seminar we manage to connect with nature and close some painful process that is preventing that different connection with life and with you.

Many couples have consulted me about motherhood, and I have the great joy of having witnessed how dozens of babies are already crawling on our planet.

Some couples have come to my office after endless disappointments and frustrations. The constellations allow us to see where those systemic disorders that prevent love from flowing into life are.

Other cases were those of saying goodbye to a baby who could not be born and whose parents' love was trapped in grief.

Parents who arrived had also underwent treatments and needed to say goodbye to the souls that could not be born.

I remember a mother who had her younger brother with psychiatric difficulties and the mere thought that her son could have the same illness was causing such fear that it prevented conception and birth.

Another case that comes to mind is that of a couple who were orphans from a very young age and the suffering they experienced unconsciously prevented them from being parents. This fear acted in two ways: the fear of leaving their child orphaned from a very young age, and on the other hand, feeling that when their child turned five years old, for example, they would be the next to die.

Answering the question that may arise…

No, not all the cases that constellate flow towards a "happy" ending if we understand it as happy in achieving our desires. We are part of a great and immense Family System and there are certain disorders or invisible loyalties to which out of love we continue to respond to. There are times when we need to work on certain topics and with such depth that the lost time is not enough to recover the relentlessness of the biological clock.

Something I often suggest to young women who are afraid that their failures in love will prevent them from becoming a *mother* is that they freeze their eggs, to remove the pressure and anxiety, thus allowing them to have the peace of mind of finding a good love. Many times, it happens that women unconsciously believe they have found that good love and it is simply a tremendous desire and love to be mothers. If this confusion manifests itself, you will see it reflected in couples who separate a few months after the child's life, or even in the middle of pregnancy.

Children

Those who have small children, adolescents, or young adults who do not leave their homes of origin and do not manage to spread their wings find here a space and a tool that will allow them to work on these issues. Here we intend to give wings to children so that they grow up in a healthy environment, be free and so their parents can also fly and be free.

Health wellness

When the topic of health is discussed, symptoms and diseases are generally discussed, but not everything is as it seems. Normally behind a symptom, or a disease, there is someone excluded from our system. In this seminar we will work on discovering and finding that what we exclude from our system comes to the surface and speaks to us through symptoms and diseases on our body. Together we will be able to let go and embrace our situation. And in this deep hug we will each find our place, and the disease its own.

Dreams and projects, money, jobs and economic abundance

How many dreams and projects do we still have to fulfill? How are we doing with the realization of our dreams and the decision and determination to take charge of our own lives? In this seminar we will all work together on those projects and dreams that have to do with the organizational and work aspects, so that we can come out stronger and empowered.

Septenniums

We can divide life in many ways. One of them is in septens. The theory of sevens is one of the pillars of anthroposophy, a line of thought created by the philosopher Rudolf Steiner, which establishes a kind of pedagogy of human life that interacts with the entire Universe.

It tells us that during each seven-year period we go through different types of fears. We have to see where we are on the timeline, but not only do we have to contemplate in what seven-year period we are and the particular fears of that seven-year period, but where we are exactly, where we are precisely, if we are close to starting a new one or to finish one.

For this, I suggest you carry out the exercise of drawing a timeline by seven years, in which you will remember important or significant events in your life. Focus on remembering and writing down (you can use a blank sheet of paper for this). Here you can detail your important moments, happy and not so happy, those bathed in successes and failures. You will also be able to understand some behaviors or situations that your loved ones went through.

Facts/Milestones of your life

Once you completed the axis with all your memories and facts, I suggest you continue reading a paragraph from the book "Vital Stages" published on Amazon Kindle (2019) that I wrote with my friend Ariel Castiglioni, and that I now allow myself to share with you.

#	Septennium	Facts/Milestones of your life
1	0a7	
2	7 a 14	
3	14 a 21	
4	21 a 28	
5	28 a 35	
6	35 a 42	
7	42 a 49	
8	49 a 56	
9	56 a 63	
10	63 a 70	
11	70 a 77	
12	77 a 84	
13	84 a 91	
14	91 a 98	
15	98...	

A septennium, as the word indicates, is a period of time made up of seven years. The first six septenniums are the most important in a person's life. From our birth until we are 42 years old, we go through stages that make up our affirmation process. During this period, we have the opportunity to find our personal mission in life and learn to live from the BEING. From the age of 42, a transformation process begins where, if we have learned to live from the

BEING, life is lived with passion and peace. If we achieve that, we could say that we will age like fine wine as the years go by. But if the first six seven-year periods were not lived in search and development of the BEING, life would transform us into an old and acidic vinegar.

Each stage of life has its own specific fears, and as an exercise we invite you to read them carefully and try to remember and identify experienced situations. Also try to identify how aggravated those situations were by the fears prevailing in said stages of your life. Before you begin, we suggest that you take paper and a pencil and write down any thoughts or memories that arise while reading.

In the first stage (from 0 to 7 years) our fear is of distance, fear of abandonment, absence, separation from parents, which intensifies when faced with the loss of a close person or beloved pet.

The second stage (from 7 to 14 years old) our fear is of closeness, fear of others, of not being loved or of not being liked.

The third stage (from 14 to 21 years old) our fear is of change, of the new and unknown that adolescence entails, the constitution as one's own person and the need to distance oneself from parents.

The fourth stage (from 21 to 28 years old) our fear is of continuity, routine and any commitment that generates a feeling of loss of freedom.

The fifth and sixth stages (ranging from 28 to 35 and 35 to 42 years old) share the same fear, the fear of losing. Losing what defines us, what we identify with, what we like to do, our sport, our time, our work, our material security, youth, motherhood, couples, marriage and others.

From the age of 42 onwards, fears are mirrored by the corresponding previous ages. If we really learned to live from BEING, life will show us one of its faces. If we could not transcend and we stay living from HAVING, then it will show us the other...

That is why the milestone of 42 years is a turning point in life. This turning point leads us, consciously or unconsciously, to a request for internal balance, which comes, even if we don't want it. We can ignore it for a while, but it always comes back, and stronger, until we finally address that complaint.

It is about looking back, contrasting what was desired at an early age with what was achieved up to that moment. And also, a look at the future, how much road I still have to go and what will be the most intelligent use and destination of my physical, psychological and spiritual energies for the second part of life.

One of the factors that helps to arrive with the least possible feeling of "existential emptiness", or as my Master of Wisdom comments, "disease of emptiness", is to start a process of self-knowledge from an early age or when we receive the courage, commitment, will and perseverance to be able to answer ourselves: why did we come to this life? What do I have to learn? What is there after death? How can I know and get closer every day to God? Who created the universe that we know? and many others.

If we do not complete part of this void with study and knowledge about the different aspects of our life, we will be distracted by searching for fulfillment and happiness externally, even when knowing that it is internally. We are going to try to move to another city or country, change our partner, buy a house, boat or new car; generating changes only externally, and thus hoping to modify our internal life. It is a very elegant way of self-deception. We know that we deceive ourselves, where the mind wins over instinct and our sensitivity.

Here I leave you some great advice, when these gaps arrive, we must stop. We must look for quiet spaces to think. Think about moments of future happiness, and then put together a plan to reach that happiness. We must have or generate the courage to go within and find the good and the bad that we have inside us.

Knowing ourselves is a tremendously powerful action to take the reins of our life and our destiny!

The seventh stage (from 42 to 49 years) is the fear of continuity. If we work on our fears and live from BEING, at this age we will not fear routine. What we will want is to transmit everything we have experienced and learned, finding a creative way to give. If we do not work on fears, instead of BEING, we will look for HAVING. This stage of life will give us the opportunity to identify what our true personal mission in life is.

The eighth stage (from 49 to 56 years old) is the fear of change. If we have worked on our interior, we will be positive by finding our security within. If we have not worked on our interior, we will look outside for what we do not have inside, and we will adopt a critical or toxic attitude.

The ninth stage (from 56 to 63 years old) is the fear of closeness. If we do not overcome our fears, we will be afraid and distrust of others, that they will harm us, causing us to close in on ourselves. The opposite of that is autonomy and social life. That would be the ideal level of consciousness for this stage. Wanting to be a useful person, listen, participate, share and open to the world.

The tenth stage (from 63 to 70 years) is the fear of abandonment. If we do not work on fears, we will demand presence. The attitude towards life will be negative and we will expect others and material things to fill our lives, demanding presence, time, energy. One can thus become selfish and even get sick to attract attention. However, if you learned to live, you will do so happily and fully.

The eleventh (from 70 to 77 years old) is the fear of losing. If we have worked through fears, we will know that with death life does not end, it is just one more step. We will not be afraid of losing, we will be like a lighthouse for others. The level of consciousness is unity, and we will worry about family unity, otherwise, unfortunately the opposite will happen.

For your information, we can also continue with the stages of life beyond 77 years of age, which, as far as fears are concerned, are repeated in correlative order.

The twelfth stage (from 77 to 84 years) is the fear of closeness, **the thirteenth stage (from 84 to 91 years)** is the fear of change, **the fourteenth stage (from 91 to 98 years)** is the fear of continuity, **the fifteenth and sixteenth stage (from 98 to 105 and from 105 to 112 years)** is the fear of losing.

LET'S START

Day 1

This magical place called La Reserva, located in *Capilla del Señor* in the state of Buenos Aires in Argentina, is a truly special place. As soon as we arrived, its silence, the natural environment, the lake, the pure air quickly connected us with the force of nature and life. Surrendering to be part of that stripped beauty was irresistible.

The afternoon welcomed us with a warm sun and spring air, which pleasantly surprised us all since the forecast announced cold and rain and we are already entering the month of the beginning of winter. That in itself was a beautiful gift.

The tranquility and magic that surrounds this splendid natural reserve seeped into the mood of each of the participants as they arrived. We all arrived from different cities, from Concepción del Uruguay to Puerto Madryn, still carrying the week on our backs, with emails to answer, work or family calls to answer, and so many more things to resolve. Anyway. The life we all live today.

As we settled in and unpacked, breathing that air and touring the place, the rings and sounds of calls and messages that consumed our energy day by day began to calm us down. Interesting metaphor, because that is exactly what we came to do with our emotional baggage: unpack and arrange.

The second step was to feed the body, essential to then feed the soul. And they were both fed. Coffee, tea or mate, accompanied by delicacies after delicacies, filled us with energy and connected us with life through the pleasure of flavors and giving us this moment for ourselves, for each other and for all of us who were there with the same purpose. Heal and enjoy without guilt or distractions.

At the end of the meal, we all felt energized, excited and ready to start working. We met in what would be our healing space for the next three days. A pagoda in the middle of the rustic and bucolic landscape awaited us. Through its numerous large windows, all the nature and the sun of a magical evening poured in.

Little by little the phones became silent, some brave people even turned them off. The noise disappeared and the sound could be heard. One by one, each found their place. We introduced ourselves one by one and thus we opened our hearts, little by little.

Presentations

Each participant shared their name and where they were from. The first thing I asked them was to, in one or two words, summarize what they expected to happen this weekend, that is, why they had given me this gift.

The words that resonated the most were:

- Nourish ourselves.
- Share.

- Leave my children a clean tree.
- Understand why what happens to me happens to me.
- Heal.
- Close stages.
- Cry.
- Clean.
- Reinvent myself.
- Check my links.
- Understand why I do what I know is wrong and don't do what I know is right.
- See what's up, I have high expectations.
- Because the constellations have changed my life, they have taken my backpacks off my shoulders and today I need to continue working on myself.

I couldn't have summarized it better. Constellate is that.

I looked around the room. I noticed that there were some beginners, also several of my faithful followers and several students in their postgraduate stages. More than fifteen people, most of them women. Good humor, openness and the desire to heal reign in the room.

I could feel on my skin and in my chest the enthusiasm of the people, their good energy and willingness. The less frequent, more nervous, perhaps more skeptical, used humor to not feel exposed and appear nervous.

I then asked each one to present the specific theme that they wanted to constellate, in this instance briefly and concisely, so that I could begin my work, which entails several layers and stages until I can properly carry out the constellation. And so, we begin.

Presentation: Woman (Septennium #9 - Age 56 to 63), entrepreneur

She has 4 children and is worried about 2 of them. However, she clarifies that some time ago, since she decided to come to the seminary, her maternal grandmother, who died at the age of 95 when she had given birth to her son, came to mind.

Presentation: Woman (Septennium #10 - Age 63 to 70), holistic therapist

She expresses concern for one of her children, in that moment I felt that there was something else going on.

"I can't move forward with my house" she adds.

"What is your house to you?" I ask her.

"My house is My Life," she answers without even taking a second to think.

"Are you leaving your life for your son? How old is your son?"

"28," she answers. I looked at her and she lowered her head.

"If you are not alive, you cannot enjoy your son or your house."

Presentation: Woman (Septennium #10 - Age 63 to 70) alternative therapies

She is worried about the second of her three children. Her life is not going well and that distresses her a lot. She adds the issue of her relationship, she says that she can't get out of the mud, they don't live together, they can't go out and have fun either, everything is hidden.

"Are you a lover?" I ask her without any judgment.

"Yes," she answers.

"Perfect" which causes general laughter in the room, I imagine, out of discomfort and taboo mixed with nerves.

"It is important that you know that by continuing to maintain this relationship as a lover you are not available for good love. Lovers are at the service of the official couples, they work for the wives and husbands," I explained respectfully.

"I also teach Reiki classes, I do many other things, but everything is always cut off due to health issues. I leave one and get into another."

"Anything else?" I asked her, and we could no longer contain our laughter. It was nice to laugh together with each other, not at the other. It is as healing to laugh with others as it is to cry with others.

"Ugh. A lot more," she adds, laughing. "Complexes, insecurities, fears, low self-esteem, and I've always had them."

"What types of complexes?"

"Complexes towards my body, towards being able to communicate as I would want with others. For 10 years I suffered enormous abuse: I felt like excrement, everything was beatings, insults, ignoring me. I was beaten once and I'm still deaf in one ear."

"How did your children deal with that relationship?" I continue investigating.

"One of my sons beats his wife, and my daughter was beaten by her ex-husband."

The silence that now runs through the room feels like a thick cold. I look at them all, and I see anguish and self-absorption on their faces. Then I explain to them that all of us who are here are because we share many of the things that are going to happen during the weekend and that we all have everyone's problems within our systems. Who has not been abused, mistreated, beaten at some point? For a family member, a friend, a son, an enemy, a stranger. Abuse, mistreatment and beating come in many forms, and there are many times that we do not realize what is happening to us. The murmur and faces indicate approval.

We continue.

Presentation of a couple: Woman (Septennium #6 - Age 28 to 35), master builder, entrepreneur; and Man (Septennium #6 - Age 28 to 35), businessman

Topic: Couple who cannot start a business

First, she explains what brings her here. She says she feels an uneasiness that has been increasing. She says it's not affecting the couple, but that she feels it. The critical eyes and comments of her in-laws make her feel guilty when they leave their daughter in their care to do something together and alone as a couple for a few hours or a few days. The comments they make are also very sexist and patriarchal, such as if she needs time to study and finish her degree, or if she does not do some household chores and outsources them.

Her voice trembles, some timid and shameful tears highlight her anguish. Her relationship with her own family is getting better, but the issue with her in-laws has even made them consider the possibility of separating. And she feels that all of this is pulling her back. The heavy burden she carries is noticeable in the anguish with which she speaks.

Then it's time to expose him. At first there is a pronounced silence. Then he shrugs his shoulders and speaks in a weak voice about the couple's projects. He says they have many, but they don't work towards any of them. He admits to having conflicts with his father and his brother that do not allow him to work well and as a team. And as a second topic to work on, he tells us that he has been biting his nails since he was little.

I suggest they do an exercise for the relationship. I place them in the center of the place facing the door. I asked six volunteers to join in and stand three to the right of him and three to the left of her. Each group of three holds each member of the couple tightly by their legs to prevent them from moving forward. Then I place a person in front of them, about two meters away, who represents "the project together." She covers her face and starts crying. He has his arms down with his hands held tightly against his body.

The "weights" on the legs represent their own paradigms and their own limiting beliefs that they transfer to the looks and comments of others: "who do you think you are opening up and doing something without us," "you don't know anything."

"The project" looks at them and says that she is locked in herself, and that she does not look at him. He first looked at him, but then he lost his enthusiasm when he looked at her with her face covered and crying. At that she composed herself and began to pull and struggle. She managed to free herself from the moorings and approached the project, but he remained motionless, unable to follow her.

Finally, and after tense moments of struggling, he too broke free and took a few steps forward.

I asked them to look at the weights they had left behind and to thank them for getting them there. I asked them how they felt. He said he felt free, nervous but free. Then he looked at her and repeated it.

He moved in very small steps towards her while she remained motionless without being able to look at him. Then he took a step back and looked at the "weights" again. How were they going to get to the "project" in this situation? He was looking back. The project looks at both of them. He turned forward again and approached her, but she did not receive him with love.

Then he asked to go back to the middle. Afterwards he asked to go back to the past, to the weights. He wants to return to mom, to dad, to what he knows. He says his body is shaking, his waist hurts. She cries. He says it scares him, and she turns toward him, backing away from him and into her restraints. They find themselves in a heartfelt, deep embrace, crying outwards a sea of old and tiring anguish.

I ask them to embrace their project together now, truly believing that they can achieve it. The tears subside into a sob and then disappear. Among the "weights" are his mother and father. The father, from the floor, looks at him proudly as if to say, "look how this asshole did it." His mother doesn't seem to like it that much.

She feels like she can't look back at the weights. The father says that he is happy. The mother says she does not believe that her son will be happy with that decision. However, "the project" says it feels that something was activated.

Looking at the field and to them I said:

"You have to be together to get here and find a strategy. Maybe for the moment and until you get off the ground this has to be your secret. This life is yours, right?"

Let's share the learning. The power of an image

In this case I chose to propose doing a systemic exercise, although it is still a Constellation, since it was going to provide us with information about what was happening. Although I could have told them in words where their problem was, I preferred that they experience it so that they would never forget it again. The feeling of feeling trapped and not being able to move is something truly desperate and seeing our partner in that situation is very shocking. This will mean that when one of you has a hard time making decisions, the simple memory of this exercise will provide the patience and understanding necessary to sustain the process that you will have to go through.

A laughter of approval and optimism erupted in the room and helped us all relax a little. It was mandatory and necessary. The air decompressed and the conversation began to flow between the participants and flowed towards the topic Lovers.

Presentation: Woman (Septennium #6 - Age 28 to 35) yoga teacher

Her theme is being a lover of a man who is not free. She says she knows that he is not good but claims that it works for her because she is dedicated to studying. When I mention the danger of falling in love, she says, "But I already fell in love." The problem is clearly one of self-esteem. Women who do not demand anything are cannon fodder to be eternal lovers. If the man goes on vacation with the woman and brings her anything as a gift, that alone makes her happy.

If a 33-year-old woman like her wants to be *a mother* from 33 to 37, it is a crucial period that is not to be wasted. If she does not find her partner, then she goes out desperately to search, consciously or unconsciously, for a "stallion," let's say using equestrian terminology. And I say "stallion" because she doesn't really love that man, what she loves is being *a mother*. Therefore, shortly after having the baby, the mother chooses the baby and discards the man, the hierarchical order is broken, the couple breaks up, and the man feels cheated.

The participant says that, from an outside perspective, she has judged the lover's role in other relationships. But now that it is her turn to be in that place, she finds a lot of reasons and explanations to justify her choice. Her career, that he is very intelligent and encourages her in her studies, that they have already distanced themselves several times but that no one interests her like he does.

She also says that she doesn't think he loves his wife, but that she doesn't know why he is with her. She is not a woman of fortune, so she is not in it for her money, they have no children, they are not married, but they work together. She concludes that they are together out of interest and because she doesn't make drama, she lets him loose. This makes me think that in this man's emotional imagination he places her libido in her (her lover), and the woman is the one with whom he feels comfortable and cared for (mother). When it is her turn to Constellate, we will delve into the topic.

We decided to take a short break to stretch our legs, get some air, have a coffee, get warm... and at that moment a participant, with a broken voice, bursts in and says that she was very distressed by the story of the previous couple. I then decided to interrupt the presentations and constellate her when she returned from the break.

Constellation: Woman (Septennium # 7 - Age 42 to 49), merchant

Topic: Reunion of a mother with her son

She looks at me. I look at her. She doesn't speak and laughs. Then I start.

"How is your relationship with your children?"

"They don't live with me anymore. The girl went to live with her father and my son went to live on his own."

She felt dejected, but eager to work, so we got to work. I asked her who in that room reminded her of her children, and she chose two collaborators. They both stood in the center of the room and just by looking at them she began to cry, covering her face. Representative *R Son* said that at first, he wanted to hug her and then he laughed, I presume uncomfortable. I asked her to uncover her face and asked him to come closer to her. He approached and knelt in front of her about two steps away. I asked them to move forward without fear and he advanced, crawling and kneeling, and hugged her legs, while the *Consultant*, upon seeing her son, let out a hurt cry and bent down to hug him.

They stayed like that for a few minutes, she couldn't contain her crying, her pain and her anguish. Then he stopped to hug her, she kissed his cheeks, and they held hands looking into their eyes. I asked her to tell her son what she felt, and she, crying, told him "I love you; I don't know why you left me." I asked her to maintain her eyes on him and repeat these words: "Son, the doors of my house and my heart, from now on, are open. My house is your house." They melted into a hug. When the *R Daughter* saw that scene, she went to hug both of them.

Let's Share the Learning: Children must go to their parents

The systemic order is that children should go to their parents and not the other way around. Children from adolescence onwards seek to differentiate themselves from their parents and one of the ways is rebellion or aggressiveness, so that they are kicked out of the parental home. This departure of the son in search of his own identity and differentiation from her could take years if it is with anger. There are times when this search is painful, but necessary to bring growth. In the future, upon becoming a father, he will begin to experience the same joys that he experienced in the role of his son, but this time in the place of father.

That is why I say to parents that we must wait for the return of life; there are times when this return is so long that our life is not long enough to see the return of the son. But children always return, even if we don't see it.

Having written the above, I give you another perspective, and that is to think that our children are giving us the space to take care of ourselves. That is why I suggest to you, dad or mom, that while you wait, you continue with your life and seek your happiness.

Presentation: Woman (Septennium #6 - Age 35 to 42) artisan

She tells us that she also has a problem with her sons and blames herself for the bad relationships she has and had with the fathers of each of her sons, both unsustainable and conflictive relationships. And she also adds that she has her house half done.

Her new partner is a relationship that is not a relationship, that is, they do not go out for a walk, they do not share dinner, nor do they share coffee. He only goes to her house for a while, stays for a short time, and then leaves. She says that she's had enough, that he has a bad side, and a very dark past, but that she never questioned it or ever talked about it with him.

So, I ask something that seems obvious but for many it is not:

"And why are you still with him?"

To which she responds:

"I do not know why."

Without a doubt, she has to be honest with herself, and clarify what she wants from this relationship and from life in general. It was tremendously striking when she said, "I never leave the boys alone with him." It was immediately clear to me that she was with him out of fear.

You meet exes when they are exes, not when you are together. When you date Satan, Satan does not like to be left. You have to decide to get out of the role of the victim. A victim actually seeks to be loved, but generates violence in others, because that victimization is violent.

If the other person is already violent by nature, any spark triggers that violence. The violent person looks for a victim, a fragile person to get the violence out of.

Internal work is essential to get out of that victim role to attract a healthy partner, no one likes to accompany someone who does not know where they stand, who does not know what they want, who does not respect and love themselves.

Presentation: Woman (Septennium #9 - Age 56 to 63), retired administrative employee

She doesn't want to make anyone unhappy or disappoint or anger anyone. Her husband is very sexist and controlling. And she accuses him of making bad jokes, she made us all laugh with her spontaneity and sweetness.

We discussed a long time ago about her boss and his "bunions," bony protuberances on his toes. Bunions form when I want to go one way and life or circumstances take me another way.

I'll tell you about her previous constellation, her boss that she loved so much died and the new boss was so bad for her that she even thought about quitting before retiring. If it were the case that a couple lives in a city and her husband is moved somewhere else and she does not want to, then following her husband can cause bunions.

Presentation: Woman (Septennium #8 - Age 49 to 56), recently retired teacher

She feels reflected in many of the people who were presenting themselves. She can't say no. She always ends up saying yes, even if she wanted to say no, and she says that's how it turned out for her. Her throat closes and her voice shakes when she says that she wants to do something else with her life now, that she feels that the time to take care of her has come. She confesses that she had a complicated marriage, from which her daughter was born from, who, as a result of her bad relationship with her father, has serious psychophysical problems.

She didn't get into another relationship, but she didn't want one either. She wanted to dedicate herself to her and have fun. And she did that for a while, but that time has passed, the time of just having fun has passed, and she feels that she must not have taken care of her in the right way since she feels that something of her is missing. She says that in her life she suffered harassment until she set the limits, but in a bad way, as they are always set when it is too late.

Presentation: Woman (Septennium #10 - Age 63 to 70), Pilgrim...lover of life

She comes to constellate the theme of the historical repetition of inadequate couples. Her first great love was an Aquarian, crazy and in love with his company. They ended up separating and each one made a life of their own. Now, years and years later, another one exactly like him arrives.

These problems happen when we have not resolved and learned what we should, then life puts it in front of us again to give us another opportunity to learn that lesson and thus grow.

I explain to her that in her constellation she should work on letting go of her first partner and saying goodbye. We have to break that cycle. Because if she doesn't, she will attract work-loving Aquarians again and again.

This same dynamic happens in all areas of life. What I have not resolved and closed is repeated.

Another example is trauma. If one had a trauma as a child or as an adult and does not work on it, resolve it or let go of it, that same fear that was generated in that trauma, when faced with any situation that takes us back to that memory or similar situation, makes that suffer return with the same intensity. Example: if as a child we almost drowned and because of that we became afraid of water and we did not resolve it, at 70 years old we will continue to be afraid of water.

Presentation: Woman (Septennium #7 - Age 42 to 49) merchant

She also brings the repetition of stories as a theme to constellate. There was serious abuse in her family that she believes she is internalizing and causing to be repeated in her own family. She also mentions that she believes there is a secret in her father's life.

Her father was adopted, and he does not know any of his relatives. When she was little, she could never count on her father, because of his job, a truck driver, he was away a lot.

He couldn't even wait for her to collect the money he had lent her, he went to her house and took everything, even the mattresses.

She has been working since she was eleven years old, and with her work she supported her family. Her first child died at 10 days old. He was the oldest. Four years later, her daughter was born and then her third son, both lived with their grandparents and not with her.

My experience tells me that when she had her daughter, she was not available for the baby, could not be emotionally present and could not "see" her as a result of the loss of her eldest son. She is in deep pain, and that is why her children needed to leave. And maybe that's the space they gave her to heal.

When she did the exercise, she couldn't see her children, she covered her face. The repetition of the stories would be: the father left, she left, because her mother wanted to take her children away because she worked all day, now her children are gone. She left with the son that didn't live. Mothers leave with the child who dies. And her parents understood that she was "gone" and that's why they wanted to take her children away from her.

What needs to be worked on is for her to love herself. On finding herself, on integrating her soul.

Presentation: Man (Septennium #7 - Age 42 to 49), businessman and specialist in international trade

First, he talks about the problems with his brother, they work together, they are doing well but he is already tired of this bond that wears out and breaks daily. His brother is more committed to the business. Meanwhile, he is getting more bored and tired every day. He wants to leave the business and do something on his own and has told him this several times, but his brother ignores him. So, he's still there and that doesn't allow him to create another story.

He also brought up the topic of anxiety, which he sees a lot in the fact that he has bitten his nails since he was very young. He is the oldest brother, followed by a nine-year difference with that brother and a ten-year difference with the youngest one. I ask him about his parents, if they live and what their relationship was like. He answers that his mother died and his relationship with his father is fluctuating. He saw that his parents had gotten along badly since he was a child, including the nine years that he was an only child before his brothers arrived.

Regarding the issue of nail biting in men, it has to do with the bond with the father. The man "eats himself" for the approval of his father.

Presentation: Woman (Septennial N°8 - Age 49 to 56), independent professional

She wants to start taking care of herself, love herself, accept herself as she is, and stop carrying others' backpacks because she knows she does it to be loved. She says that the only person who really loved her was her mother, and she doesn't have her anymore. She confesses that she was never chosen by a partner. That her bond with her children is becoming complicated. She understands that they have to fly and wants them to be independent and not have to take care of her.

She also brought up the topic of abuse; she talked about her older sister who was ten years older than her and who always mistreated her, even burning her head with boiling water when she was little. In her marriage recently she was very psychologically abused, very neglected.

She says that her youngest son bites his nails, and that her children's father is not well. She takes care of her ex as if he were another of her children. She feels alone in the world. An orphan. Her father died when she was very young, so her mother suffered a lot, and she wanted to make her happy. She even studied a career that she was not interested in to make her mother happy. But her mother is no longer there. Her only stable emotional support in the world is no longer there. She has family in Hungary, in the city where her mother is from. When the Berlin Wall fell, her mother traveled frequently for her payments, and each time she stayed a few months. She was never able to accompany her, once for college finals, once for work, once for personal reasons, for whatever reason she never went. And when she found a way to make time for herself, her grandmother dies. Because of that painful event, her mother stops visiting.

She says that for three years she has wanted to travel to Hungary to reunite with her only family and for one reason or another she is not doing it now either.

"What if I go there and they don't want me," she says with anguish.

"But if they loved your mother so much, by transitive nature, they are going to love you, you will be welcomed, and you will feel at home," I answer, giving her a little perspective.

Then we get into the topic of her children and her relationship with her father.

"Your youngest son and his relationship with his father, you don't have to get involved," I explain. "It's their issue. Because if you get in the middle, the labels appear, "dad's favorite" and "mom's discarded favorite," taking for granted a rejection from your father that may not be rejection but rather not being able to find a good and healthy way to bond with him from his own problems."

She remains silent with her gaze fixed on me and a face that tries by all means not to cry without much success. So, I continue:

"The father is going to have to change, to have a bond with his son. If his children do not go to his father, if he feels alone and suffers that loneliness and desires that contact and that bond, he will find a way to get closer to his children."

Let's share the learning: Some of my own experience with teenage children.

I look around the room and see many nodding their heads silently, and I understand that the topic of dealing with the bond between parents and children is common to many. So, I tell you about my experience, so that you can see that this happens to all of us, that it is not easy, and that everything has a time and that each member of the family requires their own process. We all have to position ourselves and we do it, or not, when the time comes. So, I tell you my story.

I went through something like that. I couldn't find a way to relate to my children because maybe I was still angry about the divorce. But I couldn't see that. Until one day my eldest son, in a moment of anger, kicked at my bedroom door. Just as I tell you. He made a hole in me! He insulted me and left. There I realized that I was not understanding something. And so, my son also got into my agenda, literally, he got into my agenda.

I decided to ask for help and went to a therapist for a whole year to try to understand and try to fix my relationship with my children. Finally, after that time the therapist scheduled us for one of his sessions and warned me: "they are going to tell you everything, but you keep quiet." So, it was. They told me everything, that I was selfish, a totally absent father with bad words as well. The therapist closed the session with a question addressed to the children: "Do you think that your father is a bad person or that maybe he has some difficulty and can't find a way to relate to you?" and right then the session ended.

We all left in silence, on the subway, I was immersed in a silence full of regret and confusion. And magically that week we got along very well. And when we returned a week later for the next session, my oldest son said that he realized that his father (that is me) had problems. And that he also had problems and that they were not going to be magically fixed because one person did all the work. It was the two of us who had to meet in the middle to fix the problems that separated us.

And that's how with ups and downs, we both began to develop the best of ourselves to maintain a very loving relationship in harmony.

Presentation: Woman (Septennium #7 - Age 42 to 49), teacher and serial seeker of tools that improve the quality of life

She opens her presentation by warning us all that she is a very intense woman. She feels that she does in a day what people do in a month. She always felt proud of being like that, because it made her feel powerful. But in that moment, she didn't feel the same way. There are days when she doesn't like to live like this, and she doesn't want all that hustle and bustle, that running around all day and for everyone. It no longer makes her feel powerful but rather tired and without a clear objective of what or who she is doing it for. That intensity with which she lives no longer gives her peace. Listening to the others, she had a thought that distressed her and closed her throat:

"But I feel like if I stop, I'll die."

I looked at her and asked her who had died recently and she said that her father died two years ago, to which she clarified that she had always been like that, since she was a child. She is the mother of two boys, and she is financially in charge of everything and now she's also caring for her mother, so she feels full of responsibilities and very little peace and fun. But she insists that what is happening to her is not new, she has already been feeling it for some time.

She says that her mother gets sick very often, adding to his children, his career, his partner who is not a partner, life has become one problem after another. She says she feels that she has a postgraduate degree in everything, but it no longer gives her pride, it no longer amuses her. She assures us that her work is good, but it is always done with a lot of effort.

She reflects for a few seconds and says that that was not what she came to constellate, but that it came out by listening to the rest.

What she came to constellate is on the subject of her partner. She tells us that she has been dating her best friend for some time now. They both play dumb because they both know things aren't going well, and she admits that she doesn't love him. But she also admits that he keeps her company and she loves him very much as her friend, since they have been friends for many years, and that is why it is difficult for her to break up. But she can't find the strength, she doesn't want to hurt him, nor does she want to lose the friendship. And she also confesses that she is not friendly with the idea of being alone, so she kinda feels like, considering the other possibility, what she has is better.

She remembers that in the constellation that the three of us did a while ago, she was crying because she didn't see the solution and he said that they could make it work. "We have, we can," he said. But for her, when there is no real love as a couple, it does not exist.

Let's share the learning: nail biting

Finally, she also mentions that she bites her nails. I see that it is a recurring theme, so I take a moment to talk about it. The issue of nail biting is a self-phagocytic behavior, which shows us that we feel low self-esteem. Let's look at the opposite. How do women look when they have long, neat and painted nails? They look super good, sexy, they take the world by storm. Nail biting is the opposite.

I remember the first constellation I did, and it was for a man around sixty years old, a doctor who was tired of biting his nails. There I located a representative for himself and another for the habit of nail biting. I could see that it was related to the distant and complex relationship that he had with his deceased father. The constellation concluded in a heartfelt and emotional reconciliation with his father. Worn nails were always at the service of reconciliation.

We will have to see in each case with whom they need to reconcile, include or let go, so that they stop biting their nails.

Presentation: Woman (Septennium #11 - Age 70 to 77) retired and happy grandmother

The issue that brings her here is her health. She has a leg that hurts and gets cold all the time. She even cut the sleeves off a sweater to make a scarf for her leg! She puts a hot water bottle on it and there are no results. She went to the doctor countless times.

"And, Claudio, do you know what he told me last time?" she told me: "And what do you want, dear! You are seventy-six years old!!" Do you think it's appropriate for a doctor to tell me that?" we laughed out loud.

We have known each other for a while, she is a magnificent woman and a very talented comedian. She is a loving person who has always taught me to take things lightly and laugh at ourselves. You could see in her eyes and in her voice how happy it made her to make us laugh.

I asked her when had she started making the "scarf" on her leg and she, in a smiling and mischievous tone, replied "when I noticed that it was becoming chronic." Another general laugh.

She, as loose and funny as she is, told us how indignant she was at being attended by the young doctor "Pablo" who told her that, when he took her on as a patient, she already had that problem, "so he was happy that, under his care, at least it had not worsened." No one could contain their laughter; her being the one who laughed the most.

"I also have another little problem," she said and paused while she searched for the words, and when he found them, she took courage and enlightened us.

"Let's say I have a stomachache."

We almost fell off the chairs from the grace that her timid little voice gave us in dissonance with her mischievous face. I let the laughter spread and die out, helping to release some tension. Then I asked her about her husband.

"My husband died of pancreatic cancer many years ago. I stopped loving him because he was mean to me. I was never afraid of him, but he was very angry with me. He always cheated on me," she said in an overwhelmed voice. "And when I stopped loving him, I was able to face him. I told him everything I had kept for myself all those years, but we always stayed together. I remember one day I told him to take me downtown to buy things and we fought so much on the way that he told me he was going to buy me a car, so he didn't have to take me anywhere else. And he did. He bought me a car! But he never took me anywhere else again. I didn't love him, but I had love for him."

Her voice was no longer mischievous, it was beginning to darken.

"I don't know why, but I had love for him. When he got sick, I just wanted to be with him, to run my hand on his back, to take care of him."

She gave us a very valuable moment. I felt how the air was suddenly filled with empathy and love flowed. Everyone loved her immediately, and I immediately knew that she would be a very important connection for everyone in this healing process.

Now it's a good time to do an exercise, we will do a systemic dynamic.

What is a Systemic Dynamics exercise and what is it for?

A systemic dynamics exercise is a simulation model that allows us to study the behavior of systems on certain problems that we provide. This phenomenological observation of the system provides us with the necessary information to broaden our view towards situations that we were unaware of or confirm certain hypotheses that we thought we had.

Both the systemic dynamics exercises and the Systemic Constellations in the hands of a good professional make the implicit explicit, allowing us to see what was not seen before.

Exercise 1: Systemic dynamics "Honor Mom, Dad and life"

The most important story I have to introduce you to this exercise is the story of my reconciliation with my father, which I already told you in the introduction of the book. There I presented the three magic words:

- **Yes** (I see you and recognize you).
- **Thank you** (for giving us life).
- **Please** (where we ask for their blessing to be able to embark on our path, relying on them and for them to give us the support to follow our destiny).

If it had not been for that exercise, which I did six months before my father died, I would never have had the possibility of reconciling with him while he was alive.

<u>Note:</u> if this order is reversed it is directed to the couple and would be:

- **Yes** (I see you).
- **Please** (let's share the path/life together).
- **Thank you** (for choosing us).

Exercise dynamics

We formed into groups of 4.

One by one they work on their systemic dynamics while the other three people take on the representation of the father, mother and life figures. Each one places parents and life where they feel. For example, one way is to place life behind the parents because life comes from them. But each one must feel with which diagram they are most comfortable with. The exercise is in silence. You have to let it flow. Let whatever comes out, let what has to happen. Then they change and now another member of the group does the work of their own systemic dynamics while the other three take the representation of the figures of father, mother and life and so on until the four members of the group have completed the exercise. It is important that the work and role changes are done in silence.

They start working. I notice that three formations are located in that triangular design and one in a line, side by side. Those who work keep their gaze for a long time. Some smile, some cry, some hold hands, and some stay serious and then hug.

One of the participants who spoke about abuse takes her mother's hand, then rests her hand on her heart, to which she adds her other hand, and then hugs her to finally push her away. She bows to her father, taking his hand with both her hands and finally hugs him. In her face I see admiration, refuge. She also makes him step back just like her mother, one on each side of life. She finally takes both parents by one of her hands and bows to all three of them. There are no tears. It is a deep acceptance of what is hers and an exhumation of forgiveness towards herself.

Exercise feedback

Some wanted to share their experience during the exercise.

Experience 1: Man (Septennium #7 - Age 42 to 49)

He says that he deals hard with the pain and guilt of not getting his brother to understand and accept his decision to no longer want to be part of the family business. His brother refuses to understand.

"I felt that my father gave me his blessing. 'You have to take care of your things and your life. I am your brother's father, not you,' I felt like he told me.

While he looked at me waiting for an answer, I asked him a question.

"Why don't you tell your brother that you're going to China for 6 months to see new technologies, and when you come back tell him that now you're going to London for 3 months to study something?"

"But this way I only continue to delay the decision..." he responded without understanding me.

"I see it differently. Your decision is already made. And it was also made explicit on several occasions. What is not there is being understood and accepted on the other side. If you do that, you will force him to get used to your absence."

He looked at me for a few seconds, thinking, then said:

"It is a good idea. It hadn't occurred to me to just leave."

Experience 2: Woman (Septennium #7 - Age 42 to 49)

"I was able to grieve with my mother. I thought it was going to be a drama, but it was nice. "Life" was fun because it was waiting for me while jogging and that amused me, because I am always on fire. But what I take away is that the other three participants chose me as their mother and that bothered me."

I looked at her with a mischievous smile and said to her (and to everyone)

"Enough of projecting that image of "only mothers" or "being everyone's mother." It doesn't help anyone or any love relationship. Let's see if we can get the inner bitch that you all have out a little! What do you think?"

The explosion of laughter and expressions of approval was contagious. Remember that there were fourteen women in the room and only two men.

Experience 3: Woman (Septennium N°7 - Age 42 to 49)

"My dad was angry because I took his life away."

I explained to her that that was correct. Because life comes from them, and they don't like us to take it without first stopping by to thank them. You will have to continue checking which issue is still pending.

Opposites come together

This drawing illustrates how opposites finally come together.

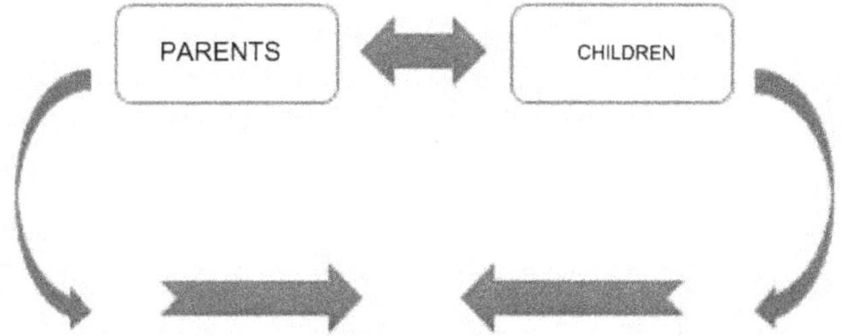

If I stay angry with my parents, I keep looking back at the past and can't look at the future. The more distanced I want to be from my parents, the more similar I will be to them, since every child has within them the sum of their lights and shadows. Life is ahead, love, projects, children, everything is ahead.

A few years ago, while constellating I was able to understand that "when we can see Light in the shadowy parts of our parents, our shadows light up and our life becomes lighter."

Exercise 2: Homework before bed. "What would my prince charming be like?"

As a homework assignment before bed, I ask everyone to write on a sheet of paper in detail what the person they would like to have by their side would be like. I especially ask to be specific and thorough in describing the attributes you want in that person.

It is very important to be specific when asking, searching and finding because, as the famous saying goes, "he who does not know what he is looking for does not understand what he finds."

The murmur quickly becomes euphoric, a product of the enthusiasm for the topic and the complicity that already abounds among the participants, and that amuses me. So, I make a personal comment:

"Be careful with exes and high school boyfriends and girlfriends. Everything that is behind, that is part of our past, is expired like yogurt, they are not the same people that live in our memories, what happened to them is life itself, like all of us who are not the same as our eighteen-year-old selves, we only have the same name since time and our experiences took care of the rest. Facebook, Instagram and other social networks are very useful for many things, but they are useless when they are used to resurrect exes.

The laughter continues, telling me that the attention needs to relax. So before inviting them to share a delicious dinner, I left them a phrase to think and dream about:

"It is absolutely possible to be happy with a good partner and have a peaceful life"

DAY 2

Another unexpectedly glorious morning greeted us when we woke up. The faint blue sky barely peeked through the cottony clouds that moved slightly through the light, fresh air. With its fresh breeze and rustic aroma, it immediately reminded us that we were still in the countryside, exposed to the wonders and whims of nature. We feel its strength bending us to accept and surrender. Mere coincidence? Pure coincidence? I doubt it.

Breakfast was a delight for the senses. It is absolutely impossible to resist the freshly made *alfajorcitos* (little Argentinean cakes) that melt in your mouth, the country bread toasts with honey or jams with their deep flavor, nor the chocolate, lemon pie, and coconut and dulce de leche cakes that take us on long journey through childhood and loves.

With full bellies and happy hearts, we prepare for a long and intense day. I feel the emotions and expectations running high in the group. Finally, here we are.

As we were settling in, the topic of expectations and anxieties came up, so we talked about it. It is important to see the role that expectations and anxiety play in our lives. When one has high expectations, or anxieties, things move away and paralyze us. That's why I recommend everyone to relax, whatever has to happen will happen. Maybe what you expect to feel will happen at the same time you expect it, or maybe it will happen at the end. Or in a week. Or in a month. The constellations work by themselves, let's say. Once the constellation is made, the system continues acting. We have to learn to be patient and do our part, which is simply being committed and connected to what we are doing and letting it flow.

As an introduction to the constellation work, we were about to begin, I shared my experience of my first constellation.

"I remember that I was afraid, panicked of what could happen. I participated in many constellations of others, and I saw them, and I remember that a cold ran down my spine just by being there and feeling that indescribable energy that united us. I saw that things were happening to others, and I suffered. It took me nine months of participating in the training course to become a Constellator to finally decided to do my own. It was an experience that I will never forget. It was within the framework of a coexistence like this since I felt that I needed more time and a lot of care."

Let's share the learning: How do Constellations work? How does a stranger feel what he feels?

Before starting I want to introduce you with some answers to the questions that people who attend my workshops and gatherings ask me.

Some of them are: how do constellations work? How can people who don't know each other feel or say things that reflect what our relatives often say? How can a stranger connect and feel what they feel?

It seems like a great mystery, but when I explain it to you, you'll see that it is easy to understand.

It all starts with a person who wants to Constellate or work on something in their life. It begins with a request that a person expresses, for example, some relationship difficulty with a child, some issue with parents, a health issue with no answers, love disagreements, difficulties at work or getting a job, etc. In short, the versatility of this tool called constellations is immense and each time more and more unusual situations or themes come for me to constellate.

Once the person talks about the problem that afflicts them, I begin to ask them some questions in order to understand something more about their life and, above all, to relate the problem to the different areas and systems that go through it.

As they tell me some clippings of their life, an endless number of hypotheses open and close within me. Until there comes a time when I don't need to listen anymore. Certain words, people and stories light up in my mind, a first hypothesis appears, and we begin to work. I tell them that what they told me is enough for me and I ask them to choose some people who will represent certain members of their family or their work or some organs of their body (depending on the system that we are going to constellate).

Once the people have been chosen, the *Consultant* who requested their constellation places them in the space (let's imagine that the work is carried out in a large room delimited by about twenty chairs forming a large circle).

The roles involved when a Constellation opens up are four. The *Consultant* (brings the topic and specific request to constellate), The constellator (me, facilitator in charge), The participants (sustain and support with their presence) and the representatives (some participants who are chosen to represent people or elements that intervene in the constellation).

In order for a Constellation to be developed, the four Roles that I mentioned above are required, it is required that the *Consultant* is clear about his/her Request (this will be clarified in the interview that we are having) and that the Constellator is at the service. Under this framework, a morphogenetic field is formed, which is a communication field that is taking shape and is nourished by the information provided by the *Consultant*'s System and is activated by the specific Request made to the Constellator.

The Constellator receives, through the *Consultant*'s Request, the Permission to be able to work with and within his System (family system of origin, current, health, work, organizational, etc.). Since all the ancestral genetic information resides in the *Consultant*, what they know and what they do not know.

It is here where the Representatives are sustained and nourished by the communication that emanates from the Morphogenetic field that, fed by the concrete Request and guided by the Hypotheses that the Constellator is following, the Constellation is developed.

At this moment is when the Representatives feel what they feel since perhaps the emotion and feelings they notice are foreign to their own.

I mention the hypothesis or hypotheses since the Constellator should not cling to a specific Hypothesis, because it is the Morphogenetic Field itself that shows us the path and flow of the Constellation. It is being aligned and in accordance with the System of the *Consultant* with the System of the Constellator at the service of a greater purpose.

One topic I want to mention is that all of us, in our DNA, have all the Systemic Ancestral information. And in a Constellation, we can access depth levels that until now we do not know what their degree of reach is.

Let's go to the constellations then, for which I will first tell you the important and useful basic data to be able to follow the process of a constellation. These are the appropriate terms used to describe the people and their roles and the different stages they go through during the constellation.

Terminology:

a) **Morphogenetic Field (Field)**: space in which it is develop, located mainly within the circle that people form when they are located at the beginning of the seminar, workshop or constellation, but which also extends to the entire space in general.

b) ***Consultant* (C)**: is the person who is making their constellation at that moment.

c) **Participant (P)**: all the people who participate in the workshop, they support and sustain with their presence.

d) **Representative (R)**: is a participant, who the *Consultant* chooses or I choose or sometimes self-invokes to take a specific role (mother, project, lies, husband, life, future, among many others).

e) ***Soul* of the *Consultant* (A)**: is the Representative of the *Consultant* during part or all of the constellation. Sometimes it may occur at some point during the constellation, that I place the *Consultant* in their own role. When that happens, I can ask the *Consultant* Representative to sit or stay. If he stays, he takes and occupies the role of the *Soul* of the *Consultant*.

f) **R=Representative of…:** You will read R *Father*, R *Mother*, R *Brother*, etc., where in all cases it is a representation of the figure being cited.

Instances in the constellation:

g) **Narration:** The *Consultant* narrates the situation they want to constellate and formulates the request.

h) **Representation:** The *Soul* (Representative of the *Consultant*) and the Representatives who will enter the field are chosen according to the problem raised.

i) **Constellation:** Beginning, where I intervene with questions and observations towards both the Representatives and the *Consultant*, creating the necessary dynamic to work on that particular topic. It is worth clarifying that many times the topic proposed by the *Consultant* turns out to be only a starting point, the tip of the iceberg, and that the dynamics of the constellation itself take us to the root of the problem where what was raised was only a symptomatic manifestation of a greater problem. The problem that can be expressed in words is often only a repetition of the original problem which can be found in another link, or in another situation and which can also come from back in the ancestral line.

Now, and without further ado, we are getting ready to constellate.

Constellation: Woman (Septennium # 8 - Age 49 to 56), retired teacher

Topic: Difficulties between siblings

She says she has a tense relationship with her brother. She loves his nephews, but her relationship with her brother is not working out. The issue of her abuse appears again: she says that as a girl her brother mistreated and hit her. He was the first man to mistreat her, then several followed.

With a voice that becomes increasingly more suffered as she talks about his brother, she tells us that he was rebellious, he did poorly at school, he did everything wrong, but that he was their parents' favorite.

"He didn't even graduate, but they always chose him anyway."

Then she talks about her mother and how much she resents her for not taking care of her. On the other hand, she feels that her father is the only one who protected her. Her father's mother died young, and her father had to assume many responsibilities from a very early age.

We begin to constellate.

I propose that she chooses one person to represent her, another her father, another her mother and another her brother. She places them on the field as follows: Her *Soul* in front of her, the R *Mother* behind her, the R *Father* far to the left. He takes the R *Brother* further away, almost with his back turned.

The Soul explains that she cannot look back. She feels alone but strong.

"He says he feels indifference" he answers, looking around.

Everyone is looking in a different direction. The only one who looks at her *Soul* is the R *Mother*, but from behind.

New slogan: I ask them to feel free, to move, to do what they want.

Her *Soul* takes a few steps diagonally away from her R *Mother* and they begin to speak spontaneously.

"When I started walking, I got curious and looked back. I see them all and they look very bad, they are wrecked. I feel misunderstood, like an outsider."

"I have chills, I want to look at them, but the trees through the window trap me. I have anger and sadness. I feel like I'm in a crappy place and that I don't receive anything from anyone," R *brother* adds.

I intervene by describing what I see and what happens in the field, and I address the *Consultant*:

"Your parents took care of him because they saw him as useless, because he was not in a position to take care of himself, he was a problematic boy. Your parents are not by your side, but they are looking towards you, they are not looking at him. Look, your brother just turned around. You come from here, from these parents, from this system. Just as you see them, half crippled, that's where you come from. You can continue looking forward or simply look at them in a more compassionate way. They did what they could. Without words, let your body express itself. Because there is nothing more than this, and there will be no more."

Her *Soul* goes out first in search of the R *Father* to express how much she misses him, thanking him for everything he did for her and what he didn't. He tells her that she has to let him go and wishes him well with her mother there in heaven. She then goes to R *Brother*, but he doesn't flinch, staying inside his angry shell.

I intervene again. I ask her *Soul* to look at her R *Brother* and tell him: "All my life I thought I was superior to you. I had a great career; I am a great professional. I achieved everything I wanted, but I'm alone, brother, and I miss you very much. Today I come to open my heart." The R *Brother*, who first looks at her coldly, from behind his shell, extends his warm and soft hands to her and answers, "I'm alone too."

I ask them to let themselves flow and they hug each other and tears flow from everyone, first removing the anguish and then bringing relief.

I look at the *Consultant* and ask her to accompany me and for everyone to take their place, mother and father behind and the siblings in front, the younger brother next to the older sister. I led them to the front, side by side. I ask them how they feel. She says well, he babbles well, but I see that her brother is quite misaligned, lost, split in half. So, I direct my gaze and my words towards her.

"It doesn't matter how much you tried before. Now it's something else. Look at your mother, she is looking away. Try to get in from somewhere so she can see you."

The *Consultant* walks towards the R *Mother*, who has her body positioned like an abandoned puppet. I ask R *Mother* how she feels, she says she can't hug her. I see that her mother suffered a lot, and I tell her about it.

"Mom's youngest brother committed suicide. But she doesn't talk much about it," said the *Consultant.*

"Even though she doesn't talk much about the subject, she is disconnected, gone, she became very invulnerable to pain."

I then ask the *Consultant* if she is angry with her mother and she answers yes. So, I ask her to tell her.

"Look her in the eyes and tell her what you need and want to tell her."

And she does it.

"I am angry with you. I am very angry because you left me alone through everything and clipped my wings every chance you had. I feel like I don't owe you anything and I helped you because it's what I have to do, because I'm a good person. I thank you for taking care of my daughter when I needed it, but you didn't take care of me. You left me very alone," she concluded in an almost inaudible, wet whisper of old tears. To which the R *Mother* responded:

"I grew by the hard way."

I intervene and ask her to look into her eyes and say the following words to her R *Mother.*

"Thanks to you I did everything I wanted, even if it was so that you could see me and recognize me. Everything I did, I did for you."

I think for a moment and share my thoughts with the group:

"Maybe if her mother hadn't been the way she was, she wouldn't have achieved everything she achieved, so sometimes there's no need to complain so much."

Now the R *Brother* goes out in search of his R *Father* and hugs him.

New formation: now the siblings, side by side, together and closely looking forward. And their parents behind them, very close to the two of them, now together. *Her Soul* is also by her side.

I then ask her how she feels now, with her system organized like this and she smiles with obvious relief and says that she feels good, the R *Father* also says he feels very good like this, the R *Mother* says she feels at peace and the R *Brother* says he is happy to see her happy.

Let's share learning: Our children and generational differences

Resolving these systems heals and allows one to seek another path, the one they really want.

I am sorry to disappoint you by suggesting with the use of this phrase that I am neither a millennial nor a centennial. I am a man of several years which I do not deny, because every day I learn something new. Furthermore, I assure you that there is no way not to say that phrase at some point in your life. That being said, here is my reflection:

"In my time we had to go out and look for mangoes because no one did it for us. Because of how much it costs us is that we want our children to have everything, and we try to give them everything. Without wanting to and without knowing we are raising a litter of kids who are different from us, who have a hard time finding out how to do it. We fell and had to get up alone. Parents before, consciously or unconsciously, were willing to pay the costs of enduring the pain and the feeling of guilt for seeing us suffer, because they knew it was for our good, to make us strong. Today our children fall, it is difficult for us to bear the cost of seeing them suffer, we quickly go out to support and hold them, knowing that perhaps this is not the best for them. They are different, they are more sensitive, they are surely teaching us a new way of being, of living, in which we can balance our lives between obligations and enjoyment. They are new generations and another evolution that, in particular, I need a little more time to gain perspective, to see my children with children and that their lives, through their fruits, show me the kind of wood on which their tree is supported, which is also my tree."

Constellation: Woman (Septennium # 7 - Age 42 to 49), merchant

Theme: A life of search and disagreements

The consultant has not seen anyone in her family for eighteen years.

"My sister and I would beat each other during fights until we bled, and my mother did nothing to stop it or separate us. My mother had an abortion, she was very unwell, but I don't remember exactly when. With the brother she got along well. My sister and I have been together for 10 years. My parents always got along badly, they didn't give each other much attention, we lived in a house that didn't have a floor," she paused sharply and continued:

"The only thing I remember about my parents are fights and sex. I remember going to sleep listening to them fight and waking up at night because I needed to hear that they were having sex to make sure they had reconciled. Everyone mistreated me and hit me. Until I left home at nineteen and that day my father abandoned me completely. I feel like they betrayed me when they wanted to take my children away from me."

"The first time the boy I liked kissed me on the cheeks, my mother abused me. At one time I didn't have anything to eat, that was when they tried to take my children away from me and I tried to commit suicide. I felt like I didn't belong in that family. I had more affinity with my dad. When they separated, I went to live with my dad in the truck."

I interrupt her and invite her to look for her *Soul* to represent her.

"Who would you be?"

Then I invited her to choose a representative for her mother, another for her father, and I asked them each to do what they wanted, to move, to find their place.

Her *Soul* walks in circles behind everyone, restless, with a severe face. The R *Mother* stood at a distance, looking down, holding her face by the chin and then by her forehead, like someone who has a heavy weight on their head.

I add a Representative and ask her *Soul.*

"How do you feel?"

"Annoyed, uneasy," she answers while walking.

I cross-question.

"How do you feel with all of them?"

"Like they are here, but they're not. I do not care."

I kept asking the others how they felt:

"I don't feel anything," R *Mother said.* The R *Father* looked at me and began to speak.

"It bothered me when I walk. I feel like I can't move. That this little square of tile is my place in the world, and that I can sink here and die in this place. When she passes by my little square of tile, I get afraid because I think that if she comes in here, the little square is going to suck her in, just like I am."

Again, I intervened and included a representative of her sister.

The *Consultant* says that her sister, ten years older, dedicated to prostitution and that when her parents saw her, they beat her badly.

"And then my sister did the same thing with me, she beat me up, just because, for fun I guess."

"You said that your mother was indifferent to the beatings you received from your sister. I see that your mother did not intervene in the fights with your sister because perhaps she could not intervene. Maybe that wasn't her real place."

I then add a new Representative to the field, without saying who or what she represents, that does not matter yet. The important thing is that she belonged there. We will know who she is as the Constellation progresses. But it was someone who I sensed was part of her system and needed to be there for her. And at that moment her *Soul* stopped wandering, and she positioned herself near her father, but looking at the *Intruding R.*

I ask the *Consultant* if she feels anything different with the presence of the new member:

"How do you feel with the new member?"

"I like how she looks at my soul, and I like that she is there" she responded smiling and blushing a little.

I asked the new member how she felt, and she said that, at first when the R *of Consultant,* her *Soul,* was not looking at her she felt bad, but when she looked at her, she felt happy.

I then asked R *Mother* how she felt about the inclusion:

"Now I feel better, like I can look at her now, but she is better far away. Closer makes me sick."

Intruder R declares that she cannot move because she needs the *Soul* to come and hug her. But it is the R *Father* who approaches the *Soul.* He first takes a timid step, then another, but then stops, leaving his arms crossed on his stomach. He lets a few long seconds pass and takes another step and ends up standing near her *Soul* and behind her. The *Soul* looks at the mysterious new member with intensity and her eyes suddenly fill with tears.

The *Intrusive* R looks at her sweetly and says:

"I can only see you now, after looking for you so much," and begins to cry. The *Soul* approaches in small steps towards the Intrusive R. That path made up of so few steps felt eternal, like a silent pilgrimage of forgiveness, old pain, involuntary absences and unconscious but tireless searches.

Once face to face, looking deeply into each other's eyes, they merged in an embrace with an uncontrollable ocean of tears of deep pain.

While this was happening, R *Mother* was approaching R *Father*, who both stood looking towards the *Soul* of their daughter going towards the arms of the R *Intruder*.

Then I invite the *Consultant* to take the place of her *Soul*, who remains at a certain distance, and in doing so begins to disarm and cry with great anguish. The *Intruding R*, also sobbing, says she can't move, that she needs her to come to her. The *Consultant* looks at me dejected and I tell her:

"It will be a matter of you starting to investigate."

Her R *Parents* walk towards her, standing one on each side, standing and motionless, while the *Consultant* loses her strength and falls to her knees on the ground. Intruder R bends down and begins to caress her back, trying to calm her down, like a child.

There everything is ordered, my first hypothesis is confirmed since there were several indications that led to the same thing, I decide to reveal and make explicit the mystery about who the *Intruder* R is, then I intervene:

"She is your real mother, your biological mother" I tell her, and now her crying turns into an endless howl of pain.

At that moment, the *Consultant* falls at the feet of her R *Biological Mother* and clings tightly to her. That cry, combusting in that infinite anguish, dissipates her, and she collapses from her, taking their entire bodies with her to slowly fall to the floor entangled in a hug and a heartbreaking cry.

The R *Biological Mother* continues to hug her, tries to calm her, contain her, but she fails. The crying is now heartbreaking.

"I feel freezing cold all over my body and I feel like I'm losing the ability to move. I'm like paralyzed and frozen" R. Biological Mother describes slowly.

The *Consultant*, still dissolving into tears and moaning like a wounded animal, snuggles tightly against that cold and immobile body as if wanting to get inside it, and ends up curled up between the legs, and remains in the fetal position. She can't stop crying, with that cry that crushes her soul to hear. Her anguish escapes from every pore of her body. And then I understood everything. In front of all of us the birth was taking place. The real birth, the one that did happen.

"That's how you were born," I told him, "From your mother, who died in childbirth."

"I'm broken," and she fell into a deep desolation where not even words can be found. She could only cry.

I continued:

"Your father brought you from another relationship, and that mother who raised you is not your biological mother. Your real mother died in childbirth."

I ask them to please help her get up and I ask the *Soul* to return to the field. I place the *Consultant* with her soul in front. Her R *Biological Mother*, always sought and dreamed of, was there, pale and with a deadly cold running through her body, but smiling, supportive and absolutely calm.

That mother was her "ticket out of that family" that she never felt was hers, she felt it too. Little by little her crying calmed down until it became a soft girlish sob.

I intervene and ask her to look at her R *Birth Mother* and repeat my words, but she cannot look at her. She looks at her hands and repeats between sobs:

"Mom, thank you for giving me life. Today I found you, and I also come to say goodbye, so that you can rest in peace, and I can also be in peace. And when it's time, and only when it's time, we will meet again. I love you. You are in my heart."

I ask her again to look at her and this time she manages to do so, and that painful crying calms down. She now looks for her *father*, hugs him and cries again. She is left hanging from him, once again with her legs so weak they can barely support her. He holds her R *Father* until she regains strength and can stand on her own again.

I ask her to stand aside, look at him and say: "Thank you for life dad, and for life in the truck," she repeats obediently, but to which she adds:

"Now I understand why you told me that no matter how big I am, I would always be your little one. Thank you."

They melt into a clearly sincere hug, expected, and much needed by both.

Now she looks towards the R *Mother* who raised her, but she does not leave the place in front of her father.

I ask her to tell her: "Thank you for what you were able to do." And I ask the mother to respond: "I did this out of love for your dad and you."

Now calmer, the *Consultant* says she now understands why there were no photos of the R *Mother* with her belly from her pregnancy nor were there any memories of her childhood.

I place the three parents in a line and face her and ask her to say to the three: "Thank you, because thanks to you I am alive." And when she finishes saying those words, she throws herself into the arms of her real mother.

I ask her to continue telling them: "From now on I rely on you three to be happy."

I relocate them all to the front, the *Consultant* next to her *Soul* whom I ask to say: "We have stopped searching, because we have all found each other."

I ask R *Father* how he feels.

"Good. I don't feel guilty anymore."

I ask R *Mother* (now father's wife) how she feels, and she responds:

"Relieved."

I remind the *Consultant* that at the beginning she had mentioned something about a secret, a secret that was repeated.

"This was the secret. It wasn't a secret about your father, but it was your father's secret about you. He was taking care of you in his own way. But now you know."

"Yes, I know. And now I know that somehow, I always knew. But now I feel very relieved. Thank you."

Let's share the learning: About Family Secrets

Several times I was asked the question: why in the case of family secrets are there times they are revealed and other times they are not?

In a Constellation the information that should be shown appears and because the System takes care of us, what is to strengthen us is revealed. Hence, a secret that should not be opened is for our benefit and it will be time for us to stop searching.

In the case of this last constellation, there were many loose ends that were not close to the *Consultant,* that she could not understand and that such lack of understanding caused her anguish, dispersion and weakness. Today her System gave her this great gift, she showed her mother and this secret that her *Soul* had always suspected, from now on strengthens her.

Constellation: Woman (Septennium #7 - Age 42 to 49), teacher, serial seeker of tools that improve the quality of life

Topic: I feel very alone

"I feel very alone. My mother had five pregnancies. Two were abortions, two were born, but one died a day later and the other a month later. They had names. Not the aborted ones. I thought I was over it, but now I see that I'm not. My relationship with my father was always beautiful, but my mother always told me that my father did not want to have children and that I am here thanks to her. I loved him very much and I didn't like her speaking badly about him. I told her that well, that she was the one who had chosen wrong, but that she should not blame it on him."

Without further ado, I invite her to choose a Representative for herself, and she chose a participant who was eating an apple. Then I ask her to choose a representative for her father and another one for her mother. While she does so, she relaxes, making jokes and sighing. Now I ask him to add her older brother to the field, and just by mentioning it she becomes distressed and begins to cry. She finally added the 4 siblings.

She places everyone behind her. Her R *Mother* approaches her, the dead daughters wander. Her parents are nearby. The R *Sister* who was born and died is located behind her father. She can't look at the R *Mother*. It bothers her.

She says that her father was never present. He worked a lot; he was the provider and on weekends he went to the club. But her mother didn't like going to the club, so she always stayed home with her. Her mother was a housewife and she retired young on what was said to be a coronary leave but which she recently discovered was a psychiatric leave.

I ask her to go and take her place. She enters the field and the first thing she says is that she feels that there are a lot of people. But in reality, what there is a lot of is death. The R *Mother* looks at the R *Father*. The R *Mother* feels the need to ask the R *Father* for forgiveness, but he does not respond.

I ask them to move where they want. The unborn child quickly moves away towards its other unborn sibling. Her parents hold hands and look only at her. I tell her to see that they are looking at her with pain and that she is the focus of their attention. She, distant and angry, says "I didn't it feel that way."

But that's how it is. Parents do many things for their children, and they don't realize it. So, I ask her.

"Don't you do thousands of things for your children and the only thing they see is how absorbed you are in your work?"

Her ocean blue eyes look at me, small tears begin to flow. She nods, but the words are stuck in her throat.

I ask her to look at them and say:

"Dad and mom, please, I ask you to take care of my siblings, because I can't take it anymore," and asks to go with her siblings.

Before going to them I ask her to express to them.

"Dear siblings, I love you, but your place is with mom and dad. Please go with them," but they say they can't.

Now the parents and the deceased sister look at the deceased son who is located closest to them. They walk towards him and hug him while the son bursts into tears because, through that hug, he feels recognized.

I ask the parents to turn to the other deceased and unborn children and point out:

"You are also our children. That we couldn't have because of fear. Today we came to recognize you so that you are never alone again. We are very sorry. You were our first and second children."

The son, in the distance, turns his back on them and bursts into heartbreaking tears.

I turn to the R *Mother* and ask her to tell her:

"I couldn't before, and now I'm here to take charge."

I ask the *Consultant* how she feels:

"I want to stop feeling guilty for being the only one who survived," she declares with enormous anguish.

I ask her to repeat these words:

"Now the family is complete: dad, mom," she pauses to contain her tears and recover her voice breaking with each pronounced letter, "and the five of us."

Her older brother approaches her from afar. Feeling him close to her she composes herself and continues repeating:

"Each one was given a role. Some was dying..." she says as she bursts into tears, but continues, "and mine was to live. At the price it cost me." At the end she adds in her own words:

"I am very happy that he is here by my side."

The second son, even from a distance, from outside the circle, says he is very angry with his mother but that the rest is indifferent to him. He says he feels good from far away but distressed. I suggest he stretches his arms out to see if there are any hugs. And yes, there are.

Once again, I ask the *Consultant* to repeat these words:

"I accept and respect your destinies, just as I accept mine. I promise you that my happiness will be your happiness. Now we are complete."

She asks permission to hug them, and they all melt into a healing hug. Feeling that company, that multitude of souls, frees her and her anguish transforms into a sob of welcome and farewell all at once.

I guide her:

"Just as you are, you turn around and now you are at the front and they support you, looking towards the future so that you can have a new change of life. This door opens outwards. I invite you to open that door and breathe in the air outside.

She does it with a river of infinite tears that flow from her eyes, fall down her cheeks, run down her neck until they get lost inside her clothes. With her last tears she would seem to be emptying the end of the enormous loneliness that accompanied her for too many years. When she turns around, her face radiated a new light, a light of peace and dedication, which shone even more when she saw how everyone looked at her with big smiles.

Let's share the learning: The weight of unborn siblings

When a person has unborn siblings, life becomes more complicated because if the parents could not take care of them due to pain, the living child, out of love and loyalty, carries them throughout life. There are times when it comes at the expense of their own happiness and their plans.

The previous *Consultant* will now have greater relief and life will surely become a little easier.

Exercise 3: The Wheel of Life and The Wheel of Relationships

I invite you to do another exercise. We make two circles divided like a cake where each portion corresponds to the following items as shown in the first example:

wheel of life

- Love.
- Work.
- Finance/Economics.
- Health/Physical Activity.
- Family.
- Personal Development.
- Fun/Leisure.
- Friends.

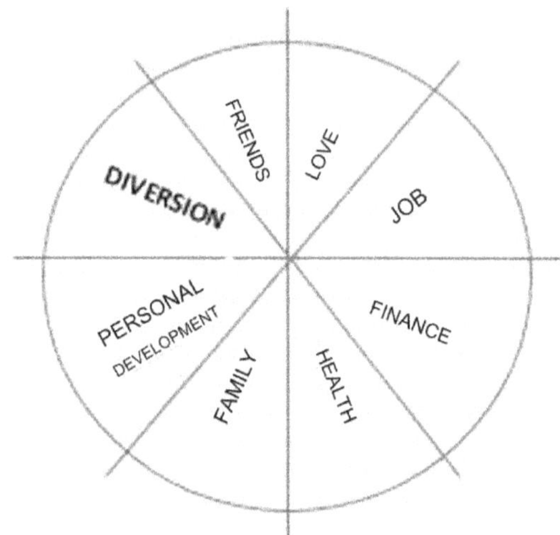

The instruction is to give a score to each area, from 0 to 10 from the center outwards, with 0 being the worst relationship with that item, meaning unhappiness and/or disconnection with that item, and 10 being the best, meaning that you are very happy with that item. Then I join the points and see what shape it has. It gives us an instant image of where I am standing.

Relationship wheel

- Relationship with my body and my health.
- Relationship with me.
- Relationship with my partners/ex-partners.
- Relationship with children.
- Relationship with siblings.
- Relationship with parents.
- Relationship with money, projects or businesses.
- Relationship with my work.

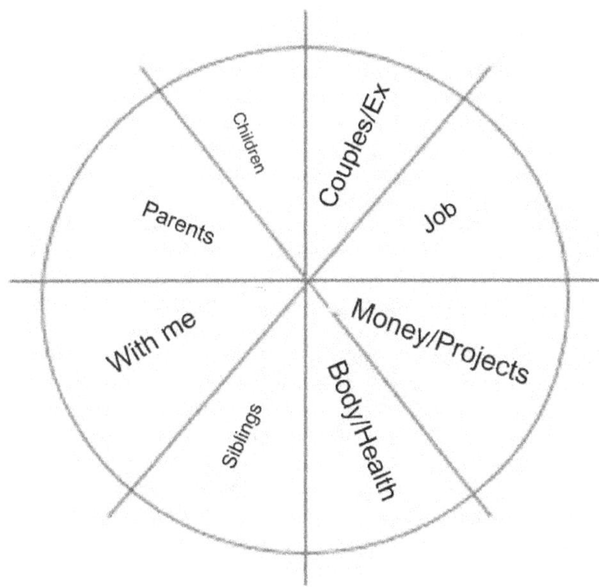

We do the same with this wheel.

This exercise gives us a snapshot of how we feel about our lives today. Which gives us a graphic way to really be able to see ourselves today and to be able to dream and plan how we would like to be in a predetermined time.

I add some questions:

- How long do I plan to live? At what age do I think I'm going to die? Write a number on a piece of paper, now, now!

- How old am I?

- What is the difference between one and the other? Do the math.

- And I ask you to write down the number and write next to it.

- What am I going to do in all these years?

When you say the numbers out loud, everyone is shocked. Some because they realize that they have many years to live and others only a few.

I put an average of 30 years and offer an example of a project, for example, a trip for each year, how do you feel about it? At that rate we would get to know the world! If each ticket is paid in 12 installments, when you finish paying one, you begin paying the other. And that helps us with another issue, finances. Why not include that trip fee among our needs and minimum income? It's just an example, although we can include more things for our income floor. But it is a plan, a project, and several projects are needed to fully live 30 more years of life. Don't you think so?

This leads us to ask ourselves how we have lived until now and how we want to continue living. Let's see a way to face this: Living from Being or living from Having.

Two models of life

Do/Have/Be vs. Be/Do/Have

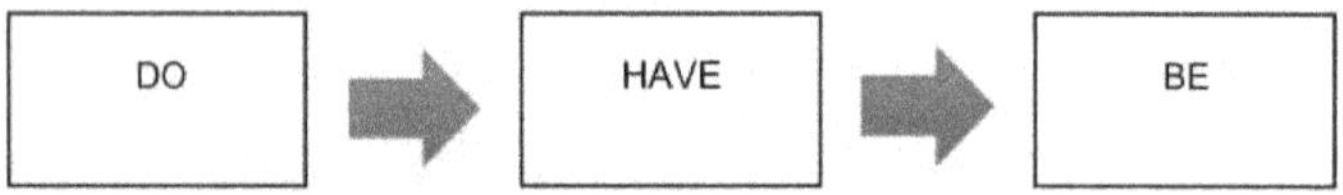

We live in a success model. In which it is necessary to DO to HAVE and HAVING to BE. This poses a destructive model because Doing to Have automatically leads me to look for systems or models that are only profitable, meaning that the only important thing is that it gives me the money I want. And if you don't give me that money, I don't achieve happiness because I don't achieve Being. Where we discard an endless number of possibilities that perhaps we like and in which we can shine and be very happy, because I learned, for example, that if I choose to be an Artist, I'm going to die of hunger. This model of Doing to Have and Being, the only thing it brings is disappointment and reinforces low self-esteem and little personal value.

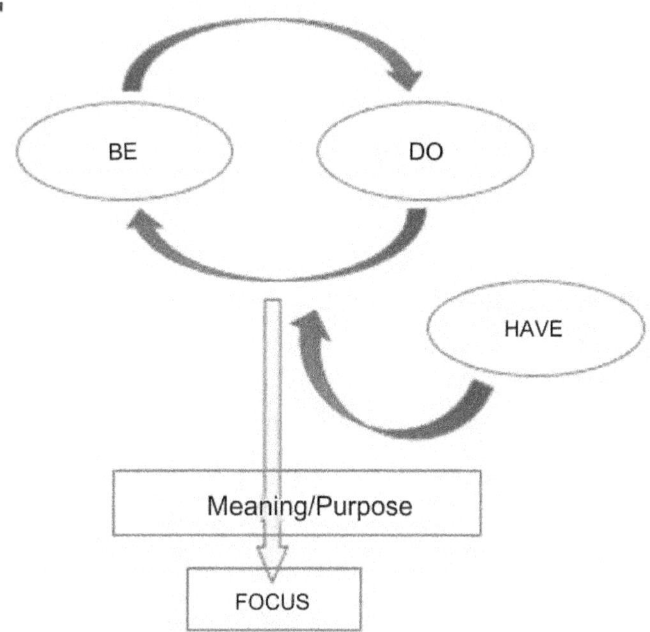

From the age of forty, where we are closer to the harp than the guitar, other thoughts appear.

It would be better to ask ourselves first: what do I want to BE? and that can determine my second life career, which has to do with what gives me pleasure, what I want to do.

I went through the same thing you go through. I had to ask myself what I wanted to be when I grew up. And I discovered that I wanted to be a Consultant, then I narrowed my sights further and chose to also be a Constellator. And to achieve that BEING, I had to DO (study and start making constellations). These DOING constellations values my BEING (constellator) and all this becomes a virtuous circle where DOING reinforces and enlarges my BEING. As a consequence, HAVE is approaching.

From the organizational constellations when I do the initial configurations, I see it a lot; who have the focus on money and therefore have it on HAVING, and who have the focus on customers and relationships, on products and services, those who are focused on DOING better in order to BE better (you can see very clearly in the graph above).

Just by looking at people I can tell if they live from Being or from Having. Living from the Being has a cost, and that cost is gathering the courage to transcend fears and manage to go through them. But it also has an enormous benefit, which is to live passionately, to live with goosebumps, bright eyes, to wake up eager to live the day and enjoy it, ready to face all its challenges.

The wheel helps us see where we are in that being in our BEING. Being in the BEING demands entering into balance. And when I sit in my center, focused on my being, my environment harmonizes.

As I said before, that doesn't mean there aren't costs. Everything has a cost. Living from the self cost me my divorce. But we must have genuine projects, from the

BEING, to give the greatest possible meaning to all the years that lie ahead of us.

Now, sometimes there is not enough time to fulfill a dream. For many it is not easy to leave what they are doing because it is what gives them the income to live. So, you have to start carrying that dream forward before leaving the system. We started doing it as a hobby until we managed to achieve an income similar to what we have at work and then we can let go. Obviously, it's hard work. It's having two jobs. The trick is to use a BIFOCAL mental lens, with one we can see up close and it is the one we use with our current job, the one that provides my main income. The lens that allows us to see from afar in the long term is what we must use to build our project / company / dream / future, but seeing it as possible and present, into which we must put our soul!

We have to put our soul and body 100% into our dream until we reach that level of training, knowledge, recognition and income that allows us to let go of the prior. That can take us between one and ten years.

I also learned that when you don't have a plan, you are part of someone else's plan. On the other hand, when you have a plan, you have the power and possibilities to choose and negotiate between different options.

But if we start at 35, 45, or 50, when you want to remember you are already with the project you wanted. What is difficult for us to understand is that time passes, and retirement reaches us all, in one way or another. When that moment arrives, it is better to be prepared with a plan B that can be transformed into the great plan A.

In a few words, I invite you to be the protagonists of your story and to take charge of your own life. The goal is not to feel trapped. You can't think clearly when you feel short of breath. Nor can we pay close attention to the country and the news because they keep us focused on the short term and this bombardment of fears does not allow us to project ourselves into the long term.

I propose that we now do an exercise that has to do with planning and goals, and I suggest that you carry out and update it every year.

My Goals and Objectives

Several years ago, I learned, when I worked in the corporate world, that just as companies define their objectives and goals in the short, medium and long term, this knowledge could be transposed to the personal world, and thus transform those personal desires into clear goals and objectives, to achieve them more easily. Since, if one is clearer about things, we become a pole of attraction for what we want.

We can work on it in two ways, the first would be that you choose and group some of the different areas of interest that appear in the Wheel of Life and the Wheel of Relationships. Another way is for you to do this exercise using the examples I suggest below.

The first thing we will do is make a brief analysis of your current situation, a snapshot of today for your different areas.

Then we will work for each area, on what you propose and want to accomplish for next year. Once you become familiar with this scheme you will be able to define short, medium and long-term horizons (this is best done for the following year).

The important thing is to start writing our wishes. If they are achievable, credible and have an end date, they will take shape and become goals. In this case the time would be a year, in my personal case I write it in December, evaluating the scope, redefining what I do not want, what I am interested in sustaining, and planning for next year.

Retrospective analysis previous year

It is the photograph of how I am, it is the analysis of my current situation and by seeing it, it will allow me to decide what things I now want to continue doing, what things I am no longer interested in maintaining, and what I will plan for next year.

In the Personal and/or Spiritual aspect

What things did I do or achieve?

What would I have liked to achieve and will I achieve this time?

In the professional and/or social family aspect

What things did I do or achieve?

What would I have liked to achieve and will I achieve this time?

In the aspect of our Activities (Jobs and Businesses)

What things did I do or achieve?

What would I have liked to achieve and will I achieve this time?

In the Economic and Financial aspect (savings and Assets)

What things did I do or achieve?

What would I have liked to achieve and will I achieve this time?

Before starting to write our goals and objectives, I need to clarify something very important. Each stage of each objective must be written in the present tense, knowing it is possible and then being able to write, also in the present tense, the next step. It should be written in as much detail as possible.

Writing with specificity, with details, with precision, very concrete, allows us to make strategies, for example, making a monthly expense spreadsheet and thus knowing in advance what I will need to invest. The same with other resources like time, and that's how I plan/project my dreams.

My Goals and Objectives for 20... (year) because I want it and I deserve it

Now close your eyes and think about next year. Take your time to Feel and Believe that a wonderful year awaits you. This year will greet you with all the good things you really want and deserve. Do you think you are a good person? Do you think you deserve to do well in life? Then have FAITH, it will happen. Now write your goals, how and what you will do to achieve them and trust! Our mind needs clarity and order to achieve our desires. Write and trust.

In the Personal and/or Spiritual aspect

What things will I achieve this year because I want and deserve?

How can i achieve it?
What will I do to achieve it?

In the professional and/or social family aspect

What things will I achieve this year because I want and deserve?

How can i achieve it?
What will I do to achieve it?

In the aspect of our Activities (Jobs and Businesses)

What things will I achieve this year because I want and deserve?

How can i achieve it?

What will I do to achieve it?

In the Economic and Financial aspect (savings and Assets)

What things will I achieve this year because I want and deserve?

How can i achieve it?

What will I do to achieve it?

Day two: afternoon

After a delicious lunch and a nap in the sun, we returned to work. Energy was running high as were emotions.

The last *Consultant* who constellated, asked to speak and tells us that she is on her period, but that after her constellation she noticed that the color of her blood changed, and she began to have very strong pains like labor. And the feeling she had was that she gave birth to a son. It doesn't catch my attention since few people have the possibility of relieving their own birth. So, this seems to be a replica of her body's experience of what she experienced in the constellation. My reflection is that this is just the beginning for her. Maybe it was time to go see her father and seek that reconciliation. When systems are constellated, they begin to compensate in a way that is difficult to understand because they operate in very vast forms and spaces.

Where do we look? Are we clear about our place within the family?

You think you're looking where you say you're looking and then you wonder why things don't work out. Are we really looking where we think we are looking? Are we clear about our place within our family? We believe that as children we are placed below or in front of our parents, but are you sure that is the case? I see every day in each initial image of a constellation, that people believe they know what their place is, but unconsciously, innocently, out of love and loyalty our soul occupies a place that is not ours, a very important part of people maintain their own parents from a place of Custodians. And the Custodian is at service and does not have permission to live their own life, they do it through whoever they guard.

In the graph you can see yourself in the center circle (VOS), above I placed 4 joined arrows that indicate the possibility of where you can look. We can be looking at a single place or at several. The more dispersed our gaze is, the more difficult it will be to concentrate on our future, on our children, on our projects. That is why it is so important to free ourselves from burdens and resolve unresolved issues with our parents, siblings, partners and ex-partners.

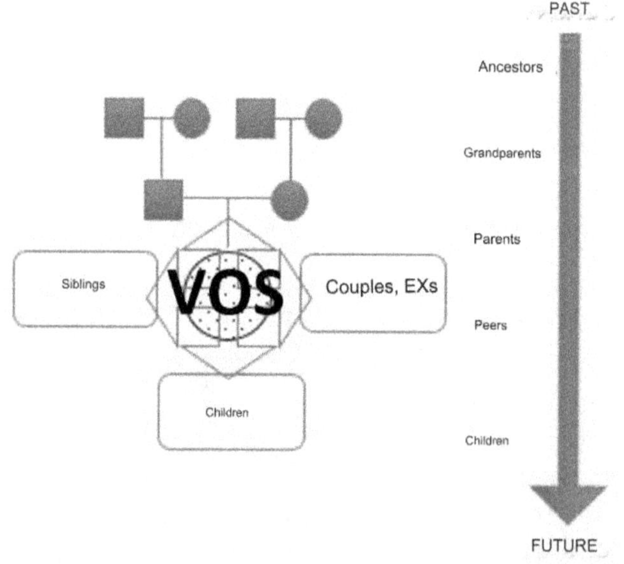

If I'm thinking about an ex-partner then I have it in the future, rather than having it in the past. So, if my future is occupied by my ex, there is no space or energy for a new partner. The same with parents, they are in the past, siblings and partners are in the present. In the future are children, projects and, if there are any, new partners.

This only serves to organize where I am looking, and therefore where our energy is placed and whether or not we have availability for what we say we want.

Constellation: Woman (Septennium # 10 - Age 63 to 70), Alternative and holistic therapies

Topic: Finding a good partner

Her list of topics to constellate is endless. So, to achieve the greatest efficiency and effectiveness in the constellation I ask her:

"Where do you feel that your life hurts?"

Strong answer.

"The couple."

I ask her to read her assignment of describing her Prince Charming. And the list of specificities was as long as that of the themes to be constellated.

"How many important men were there in your life?"

"Only one."

"Which?"

"A man who I fell deeply in love with after my husband. But we are over."

"Because of him?"

"No, because of me. I've always been the one to cause the breakup. I've never been broken up with," she says proudly.

"How many years were you with your husband?"

"Ten."

Now I begin to delve deeper into her primary relationships.

"How was your relationship with your parents?"

"I don't remember having any problems until I got married, then my mother made me feel like I had hurt my entire family because I got married at 17, pregnant, and he was an opportunist. I feel for him, I loved him, but it was a great suffering for my mother. My father was the only one who told me that if I didn't want to get married, I should have told him. But my mother said there was no option for me except getting married. And well, here we are," she explains with resignation.

I ask her to choose the representatives: hers, her children's, her mother's and her father's, and then I ask them to place themselves wherever they want.

"Did you have any loss of a child?"

"Yes, my husband forced me to have an abortion. Well, I had two."

"Who would represent those two children who did not get to live?" she chooses them, and they enter the field.

The R *Husband* moves with his fists clenched, walking angrily in small circles.

Her Representative, whom we call *Soul*, feels a tie in her legs that is why he kneels. She feels pain in her genital area, and she says that her husband also raped her besides having been raped in childhood.

She cannot relate to her R *Husband* because she feels anger and a rejection that does not allow her to turn around and look at him. I ask her *Soul* to turn around and tell him NO. Her *Soul* cannot.

I ask her to tell him: "I loved you," but she asks to say something else, so I invite her to say what she wants.

"I had an illusion and you destroyed it," I intervene and ask her to change the word "destroyed" to "killed."

"You killed it." She speaks.

After those words the *Soul* gains strength, stops kneeling and stands up facing him. And it is perfect because to look at others you have to be at their level.

"I need to look at them both," she asks me, referring to her parents. I intervene and ask her to say:

"Dad, I ran after an illusion," she adds.

"And made a mistake." She explains that she feels that her father was not there for her, nor was her mother. I intervene:

"They couldn't" to which the *Consultant* confirms that yes, they couldn't because they were from the countryside.

"I took a risk on my own, you had nothing to do with it. I would have liked you to be there anyway."

I intervene:

"Now you can, come closer."

She approaches but doesn't look at him. He puts one hand on her shoulder, she remains still for a few seconds and rests her hand on his.

I look at the field. Mother R stands with her fists clenched until her circulation is cut off. I ask her how she feels.

"I feel like I'm made of stone, and I can't say anything."

I intervene:

"Can you look at her?" The mother turns her head, and her gaze is full of anger. I intervene:

"What do you feel?"

"I feel like I want him to slap me hard. I feel drowned in anger."

I direct my gaze to the *Consultant*, who is restless, and ask her:

"Did your parents have a violent relationship?"

"I don't remember."

Here appears an important concept called Double Transfer. This occurs when a mother mistreats her father; her daughter, out of love for her father, goes out to look for a man who mistreats her as if it were a kind of offering to her father.

"You put your body to defend your father, and you took the blows to defend him."

I ask her to look at them and say these words:

"Mom and dad, your issues are yours. And I have nothing to do with it. For the love of dad, I put myself in the middle. And relationship issues are resolved by the couple. From now on I will take my place as a daughter."

I ask her to stand closer to her parents, in front of her mother. She wants her *mother* to talk to her, she doesn't, but she changed her posture. She is no longer with that arrogant posture, she is unarmed. It is the *Soul* who approaches the R *Mother*, kneels in front of her. Finally, her mother breaks down and hugs her and they both join in a cry of old grudges melting away.

Now I ask them to sit up and for the *Soul* to tell them:

"Thank you, mom and dad. More than sixteen years of life await me, which I want to enjoy."

The R *Husband* wants to leave, but I ask her to stop him and tell him:

"Thank you for the children you gave me, for making me a mother. From now on I release you and free myself so that we can be happy."

I ask your *Soul*:

"How do you feel?"

"Good, although I feel like crying a little."

And she cries. She cries absences, disappointments, loneliness, fears, and abandonments.

While this happens, I make a new representative appear, the Love that awaits her. I intervene:

"The beatings and the suffering are over. "And I invite her to join him in a hug. "Go! Get in! That is the love that is waiting for you! Grab something!!"

Wiping away her tears, she begins to laugh, and we are relieved with a good laugh that we sorely needed. And while she, between laughter and tears, settles internally, I add:

"One more thing, leave the lover. Nothing will appear as long as you remain in that situation."

Let's share the learning: There is no age to fall in love

Many times, people come to my office who want to find good love and in all cases I observe that their gaze is directed elsewhere, as we witnessed in the previous Constellation. When the gaze is directed elsewhere, the person is not available and the only thing that THEY attract are unavailable relationships.

The Constellation allows you to free yourself and generate the space that I call "availability for love." Only when you are available will you be in a position to attract a love that is also in the same circumstance and that will be waiting to find you.

There is no age to fall in love and we should not lose hope of doing so. We were born to be in a pack, in a group, or simply be in pairs.

Constellation: Woman (Septennium # 8 - Age 49 to 56), independent professional

Topic: I feel like I can't move forward in life

"I feel unbalanced in every way, and I cannot move forward in my life in any aspect. I thought I would constellate the topic of my sister's abuse that I already mentioned and where my mother was my refuge. My mother died very young."

"My dad spoke Hungarian, I was little, but I don't remember him ever speaking to me. He left when I was 4 years old. Then my mother married three times, and her third husband stayed until her death, he was the one who raised me. They told me that my biological father had died. When my mother died and I had to take care of the estate, I found the death certificate. When I was 6 months old, my mother had a stroke, and she was hospitalized for 6 months. My sister and I were left in the care of one of my mom's friends. She later recovered, but she remained hemiplegic. I'm afraid of my sister. I have been afraid of her since I was little, and I am still afraid of her today. I almost never see her, only for family succession procedures. They gave her the land where her house was built, and I gave her all the furniture in my house. But when mom died, she forced me to divide everything equally. I think my mom felt guilty about my sister. When I wanted to travel or the possibility of going to live in another country arose, my mother was happy for me. But my ex doesn't like to travel, so I never traveled. And now I really need to travel."

"I feel like you're angry because they gave her more things than you."

"No, I'm angry because she's ungrateful. She couldn't tolerate my mom. I told my sister to reconcile with mom when she was already very bad because she could die and then she would regret it and she did. But we never managed to reconcile."

I ask her to choose the Representatives of her, her mother, and her biological father, her mother's first husband, the third husband who raised them, and her sister."

Everyone gets situated, and then I ask her how he feels.

"I feel very hot. I don't want to be here, I feel suffocated. I had chills when my sister passed by, and her father made her want to throw up."

Now I chose a Representative of her ex-husband and asked him to locate on his own, then his youngest son and to locate on his own and his eldest son and I also asked him to locate on his own. I observe and intervene:

"Look how your mother leans on you."

Sitting in front of all the Representatives in her life, tears begin to flow. Her *Soul* moves restlessly. I bring two pillows, I throw them in front of the representative.

"Come on, unload."

His soul looks at me angrily and tells me:

"I feel like I want to kick them," to which I respond:

"Do it then." (she kicks them)

"I feel like I can't take it anymore, that I'm about to lose everything. I want to go there, with dad."

"Go then, hug him, because he is excluded."

They hug each other crying and his father declares:

"I love you."

"Interesting, you can listen to it in Spanish."

I intervene again and ask the *Consultant* to go hug her R *Father* and herself, her *Soul.* The three of them hug, then the R *Mother* moves to one side of her, leaving the *Consultant* and her R *Father* hugging. Her R *Father*, with tears streaming like a waterfall, whispers words of encouragement, approval and love. She thanks him, holding his hands tightly.

Now the R *Biological Father* approaches the R *Father who raised her*, her mother's third and final husband, hugs him and gives him a magic word:

"Thank you."

Her *Soul* speaks and affirms that she does not feel guilty about anything.

I intervene, and ask your *Soul* to say:

"I am me and I shine by my own light."

Now it is the R *Sister* who asks to speak and crying she says that it is her sister who is lucky because someone told her that they love her, and no one ever told her that.

The biological father stretches out his hand looking for his partner of so many years and holds her close to his side.

Now I ask her *Soul* to turn to her older sister and tell her:

"I accept you as my older sister, but I no longer accept any more abuse."

The R *Youngest Son* approaches. The R *Eldest Son* says that he can't stop looking at her with fascination.

We close the Constellation with the sister.

"And your ex?"

"It makes me want to say, 'come on, you fool, come here!'"

"Then tell him."

I ask the *Consultant*:

"What would you say?"

"That he was a great life partner, but that I no longer love him."

I intervene, and ask her to say these words to him:

"Thank you for all these years, for the love that existed between us, for making me a mother and for our beautiful children. It was a shame this couldn't continue, but that's life. From now on, I release you and release myself with love so that we can be happy. "We will always continue to be the parents of our children."

I ask her to breathe, stretch, and ask her how she feels.

"With another voice, with another strength, good, peaceful."

But his R *Eldest Son*, from far away, said he felt disoriented. I intervened and asked the *Consultant* to approach him with love, look him in the eyes and with deep respect say these words to him:

"I no longer feel love for your dad. And for my own dignity and for his own dignity, I decided to separate us. You have to understand that for your own life; that, if they don't love you, they don't love you. And if they love you, they love you."

The R *Eldest Son* says that the separation does not make him angry, but that while everyone is settling in, he doesn't know where he should be.

I intervene and tell the *Consultant* to place him in front of them. So, in the new formation they remain: R *Eldest Son* and R *Youngest Son* are in front of their parents.

And I asked her to tell the R *Eldest Son*:

"This is your place, in front, not to the side, you are not a peer, you are a son."

I also tell her that she has to explain this dignity thing to his Eldest Son, because of his girlfriend issue. Because he is with someone who doesn't love him.

I look back at the formation and explain:

"Your father appears now in your thoughts because the father is the exit to the world. When you went to look for your father, all that crowd of people opened up, it cleared up a little.

Finally, the R *Mother* told us that when her first husband, who had died, appeared, she felt very bad. But luckily the *third Husband* appeared who, when he took her hand and pressed her against him, felt love, peace, that was flying. That was the man who raised his daughters. And it turned out that he was also the greatest love of his life.

Let's share the learning: Every woman has 2 births for each child

All women have two births for each child. The first is when her son is born and the other is when she gives the son permission to go with her father. It is enabling her son to stop being a boy and become a man, which he can only be if he goes to his father. If this does not happen, the male child remains with his mother, depriving himself of the ancestral masculine strength that is only found behind his father. The healthiest thing for the son is for his mother, with all her love, to step aside and allow her son to bond with his father to become a man.

Constellation: Woman (Septennium # 11 - Age 70 to 77) retired and happy grandmother

Topic: Health (breakdowns)

"Well. Tell me."

"I do not know where to start. From the beginning they say. When I saw one of the previous constellations, I realized that I never made a constellation with my family. For example, the things that happen to my son are unbelievable."

"Like what?"

"He was in a relationship with a girl who had a daughter that he took care of and in the end, she left him. And they had a son together. I told him that he should help her because when you have children, the man has to help the woman. But it turns out that if he didn't clean, she didn't clean, if he didn't cook, she didn't cook. And one day she kicked him out in such a way that he showed up at home with his things in garbage bags. And my husband never worked."

"What else caught your attention about that Constellation you mentioned?"

"I realized that I can help my son. My daughter is fine, she can take care of herself."

"How old are your children?"

"They are adults."

"What was their relationship with their father like?"

"The father always humiliated him."

"What is your son doing?"

"He is a policeman. But he doesn't get called from other places. He is looking for other things, but he doesn't find anything. He came to live with me. He doesn't bother me because I have a big house."

"Okay, but we're trying to solve his problem and he has to take care of that," I remind her. So, I continue investigating.

"Well, let's see what we can do so that your son can also benefit from your constellation."

"Yes, my daughter is more independent."

"Yes, women are like that. They don't need us. Except for making barbecues," I added smilingly, to which all the women responded in unison:

"SOME!!" inevitably there is general laughter.

We then begin the constellation. Without forgetting the main reason for the consultation, which was her health, her breakdowns and constant and permanent trips to the bathroom, which she had mentioned to us on the first day. I ask her to choose a representative for her *Soul*, her mother's R, and her father's R.

"How do you feel with them?"

"Fine, I guess, when my dad was there you couldn't answer or say anything. How was I able to get along with him? Meanwhile to my mom I was everything."

The R *Mother* seems lost, she walks aimlessly and dejected. The R *Father* is standing tall and hard.

Her *Soul* faces them, but with love and says that being there with them like this makes her feel good.

We add R *Husband*, who also doesn't find his place. His *Soul* is fascinated with that father, the rest does not catch her attention or move her. Now the R *Son* appears. When the son arrives, the walkers stop, and he places himself between her and the R *Husband*.

I add another Representative that I do not identify, but whom I ask to come in and settle wherever they want. Her *soul* is still fascinated with her father, and everyone is oriented towards him.

Carefully observing her Constellation, the *Consultant* comments:

"He was rude, I was not fascinated by him."

I had been watching her. She kept her smile on for a long time while she moved restlessly, but her face gradually lost the smile until it disappeared. Her face was now tense and attentive, and her body now remained still, expectant.

I add a new hidden Representative who locates themselves between her *Soul* and her *R Father,* but maintaining their eyes on her, on her *Soul.* But now her *Soul* loses its fascination with the R *Father* and her attention and curiosity move intensely towards this new Representative, who functioned as a tension filter and relieved both the R *Son* and her *Soul.*

The R *Father* says he is curious.

Before the restless eyes of everyone, I reveal the identity of the new Representative. It's the R *of Fear.*

"The first hidden Representative that I introduced was looseness of the bowels," I confess, and I felt how her attentive and deep gaze devoured the information. Then I continued:

"Before starting your Constellation you had to go to the bathroom. Look at the field and let's observe together how your Constellation now develops. The problem of going to the bathroom continuously is in the middle of everyone. Fear has now gone to look for you and embraced you, it is taking you to the origin of your fears. It doesn't take you with violence, it takes you slowly, with respect. To face it face to face."

I ask her *Soul* to look at her R *Father* and say:

"Dad, today I come to see you, accompanied by my fears."

I ask the father how those words make him feel and he says he doesn't feel anything, just something heavy behind him. The R *Fear* now moves behind the R *Father* and holds him.

The father was afraid of things he did. Like a bad dog. And people knew it. Out of love you carried his burden. I ask the R *Father* to look at her and say:

"Dear daughter, thank you for the great sacrifice you have been making for me by carrying my fears that are not yours. I take care of them and free you from all burdens." Her *Soul* claims to feel strong, good, but her voice is muffled.

"The looseness of the bowels has retreated, because it takes with it the fears and burdens that are not yours. Her *Soul* does not feel like hugging her R *Father*, she says she is fine like this. I ask her to just say: "Dad, I ask you to please take charge and from this moment on I give you my looseness of the bowels and cramps. Thank you.""

I ask her *Soul* to retreat back so that the problem of going to the bathroom can re-enter and take the father away. So, what your father ordered is for him to take with him. He says he feels relieved because it's like a weight has been lifted off his shoulders.

Her *Soul* asks to move places and stands in front of the R *Mother*, gently takes her arms and surrounds herself with them, leaning on her chest. The R *Husband* is distant, but finally he reaches out to her *Soul*. She looks at him with that sweet firmness that characterizes her and addresses him these words:

"I put up with you until the end since you are the father of my children."

I ask her how her son is, and she responds that he looks fine.

"Now tell him: Dear son, your place is in front of us."

I ask how the son feels, and he replies "Great."

I pause while I observe her and I turn to the *Consultant*, who is reluctant, not reacting, and I ask her:

"How are you?"

"Good. But you didn't put my daughter."

"Since she takes care of herself, I didn't put her in, but now we can put her in, so we complete the system."

And then the R *Daughter* appears. Now I turn to R *Brother* and ask him to stand in front of his R *Sister* and tell her: "Sister, I am the eldest, and you are the youngest. That is my place and that is yours." Then I invite them to change places, but the *Consultant* does not like it. And neither does the R *Son*. He feels uncomfortable. And it is fine. Changes cause discomfort.

I ask the *Consultant* again:

"How do you feel now?"

"This should have happened a long time ago," she responds, her voice breaking.

Again, I turn to the *Consultant*, who is now clearly mobilized, and I ask her:

"Go give your mom a hug."

The *Consultant* stands up, walks quickly towards her and collapses on top of her crying loudly and without shame. With a broken voice she acclaims:

"Mom, I miss you so much! I'm lost without you."

I intervene, I ask her to stand in front of her R *Mother*, empower herself with her love and looking into her eyes tell her:

"Today mom I come to say goodbye to you so that you can rest in peace and so that I have peace. And when it's time, and only when it's time, we will meet again. I love you."

She falls into her mother's arms again. Finally, I ask her to tell both parents:

"From now on I rely on you mom, as I always did, and on dad to be happy."

The Soul is placed next to the *Consultant*, empowering her and tells her "And with you we are going on a trip, because I left the looseness of the bowel to dad."

Let's share learning: Meeting points between two systems (the body itself and the children)

What you may have observed in this constellation is that during the interview I let the *Consultant* talk about several things. I was clear that health and her urgent problems with going to the bathroom, were the problem to constellate, but I also felt the concern that the *Consultant* had for her son. Allowing it to spread was intended to find some meeting point between the health problem and her children, so we worked with them to free them as well.

In this case we can see a health problem of the *Consultant* that came as a consequence of taking charge of the fears that were present in the system when the victim/perpetrator dynamic was active, this means that someone from the past was a victim or perpetrator and that that is not resolved passes to the next generation, transferring the problem. In this case, the *Consultant* brought it from her father, with her occupying the role of victim and also her own son. Now it will be a matter of observing over time how the *Consultant*'s son is hired to do other work that is not policeman and that the bathroom problems are removed forever.

Constellation: Woman (Septennium # 6 - Age 35 to 42), artisan

Topic: Desire to be happy and have a good love that values her

We remember together the two times I saw her.

"One that you were in a couch sitting there in the back, you could hardly be seen. And then the second time you looked divine in a beautiful outfit that I didn't even recognize you. Where are you now on that spectrum?"

"There, but they want to see me here."

"Stop, stop, stop. It doesn't matter what others want. It's about what you want."

"Yeah. You are right. My problem is the issue of my children. You said that children have to be there and need their father. And I have problems with the fathers of my two children. And as you know, I'm going to be a grandmother. My daughter is pregnant, and she is afraid of her father, but she told him. My youngest son is the one who suffers the most because he is in the middle of his father and me. And my other son is with his father. Ultimately, I want fathers to take care of their children. My daughters are like me, they are not going to be screwed. And men are not like that."

"And what are you going to do?"

"Let them go."

"That's very good. And the parents, do they take charge?"

"No."

"Then how are you going to do it? Let's get organized. Two children per father."

"Yes, but my last partner threatened that if I left him, he would commit suicide. And I couldn't leave him at that moment because my father committed suicide. And I didn't want my children to go through what I went through."

"And? Did he commit suicide?"

"No."

"Can´t you see? Nobody commits suicide for love."

"But he won't give me any money if I don't give him any indication of returning to him."

"You have to solve that with a lawyer. The money belongs to him. You solve that like this. There is no magic, no shortcuts. It's like that. Now. Let's see how you are. Let's constellate."

Her Soul, the R *Father* and the R *Mother* appear on the field. I asked her to place them however she felt. She placed herself in the middle. R *Mother* behind on the left, and R *Father* behind on the right.

She moves and stands behind her dad. I look and tell her:

"Do you know why the things that happen to you happen to you? For the love of your father that you held, taking the place of your grandparents. You are occupying the role of Custodian of your father. This is how you become invisible. You go to his world. And there is nothing for you there, you are in the world of the dead."

From there I ask you to say these words to your father:

"Dear dad, now I can see that for love of you I am holding you in the place of grandparents. But this is not a good place for me. That is why, from now on, I leave the grandparents in this place to settle in my place."

I ask her to breathe and move forward. I incorporate the figure of the grandmother and grandfather behind. Now I ask her *Soul* how she feels, and she says she feels a little better.

I now add the R *Father* of *her first two children*, who located himself in line with her on the right, and then the R *Father of her two youngest children*, who located himself on the same line as her on the left. Finally, I add the four children, all of them stand before her *Soul*.

I invite the *Consultant* to take the place of her *Soul* and ask her to look at the R *Father* of *her first children* and ask her to speak to him. But she bursts into tears. After a few minutes she composes herself and repeats:

"I loved you, and I chose you to be the father of our children. It was a shame that everything that happened did. But that's life. And today I release you and I release myself with love so that we can be happy. We will always continue to be the parents of our children. And I ask you to please take charge of the role of father. Thank you."

I ask her to breathe, and if she feels it, to say goodbye in a hug. She takes a deep breath, moves forward and hugs him, containing her grief. I ask her how she feels and with a broken and almost inaudible voice she responds "better."

The *R of the Sons* feels better, more relaxed.

Now I ask her to speak to the other father and repeat these words:

"I do want to be happy, and I know how to be happy, and it is my decision not yours, I don't love you anymore. And I ask you for my dignity and for your dignity as a man to accept this reality. I chose you to be the father of our children. And that's just what you're going to be. I ask you to please take charge of your role as a father because the children need you. I release myself and I release you with love so we can be happy. Thank you"

I once again suggest that she breathes and gives him a hug goodbye and with that she will lose his understanding. I ask her how she feels, and she says "better," but it was almost silent.

I ask her now to look him in the eyes and say:

"Your place is on this other side, because you are part of my past."

I send the *R of the Children* to order, everyone complains, but she orders them with love. Then I ask her to look at them and say:

"Dear children, do not worry about us anymore. Couple issues correspond to the couple. Go play and be happy, because your mom and dad love you, take care of you and protect you."

Now I ask everyone to look forward.

She keeps talking about exes and children, so I stop her with authority.

"Stop looking there! That's your past. Focus on your future."

I asked her to repeat these words:

"I'm organizing my system. I just said goodbye to my exes, and now I'm available for good love. Thank you for waiting for me. Now I am available to find my good love."

When she finished the words, she started to cry, and at that moment a New Representative voluntarily entered, who introduced himself as the representative of love. He went straight to her and hugged her.

"Look at you," I joke to the *Consultant*. "Only the sweetheart came in!!

We all laughed and laughed and continued joking with her.

At that point she meets my gaze and holds it imploringly for a few closing words. So, I close it:

"You're going to go see the lawyer, resolve the issue and stop victimizing yourself and playing dumb! If you want, I'll tell you in English, which sounds better!"

Laughter exploded, and the loudest came from her. How good it is to laugh with others. And even better is to laugh at yourself.

Let's share the learning: Your own power

Where do you think your power lies? In others or within yourself?

We all have the power to decide how far and how long.

Do not fear rejection, since pleasing has a much higher cost. If you seek to please, that is where you gave your power. If you seek to be yourself and be happy with who you are and what you do, the power lies within you!

Constellation: Woman (Septennium # 10 - Age 63 to 70), pilgrim...lover of life

Topic: Stop repeating stories with men

"Well, my theme is repeating stories. I was with a person for 7 years; he went to have a heart study and he died. And it's happened to me before," she explains to us with a certain tone of resignation.

"You know it does, sometimes it happens. I have a friend who was chosen by five men and then died in her arms. The last one was given a terminal diagnosis and he committed suicide."

Not a fly flew, the air became tense and expectant. She continues:

"Yes, I was very bad for two years after that. I found another good man, all very good men I had. One day a friend introduced me to a man, we got along, we had plans to unite families, retire, buy land and we built a beautiful cabin. In the middle of that he tells me that he feels a pain in his leg. They found a tumor in his leg, and he fought it for 7 years, but three years ago he passed. Now I want to sell everything, my daughter is in La Plata. I travel there for birthdays, I traveled last year, but I want to share, but I always end up alone."

She pauses in the total silence, breathes slowly and long, and continues:

"I want to find a person who wants to enjoy life, to travel, to take walk, to read a book, to drink a good wine, to eat a piece of cheese, to stare a starry night...I don't know. That he likes to enjoy life, that he wants to and that he can."

At the end of the sentence the other participants energetically claim:

"I also want that!"

To locate myself on the timeline I begin to investigate.

"How many men passed away?"

"Two"

"Is one of them your husband?"

"No, he is alive."

"Tell me about your family."

"I am the seventh of ten siblings."

"How was your relationship with your father?"

"At 9 years old I confronted him because he was an alcoholic, he was very aggressive with her, and I couldn't stand it. My mother was already very old. I saw that she was repeating history, and I didn't want any more. And I want to know why this happens to me with men."

We chose representatives for her and for the two men who passed. I ask them to find a place to stay on their own. I distinguish which was true love, I share it with her, and she nods.

I ask your *Soul*:

"How do you feel?" But it is the *Consultant* who answers energetically.

"Attracted."

We burst into laughter. Fiery The *Consultant*!

I suggest one of the men for her *Soul* to start with, but she chooses the other. I ask her to look at him and repeat:

"Thank you for the good moments we shared. I carry you in my arms."

She left the other man for later for a noble reason, he was her true love. So, I asked her to tell him:

"You were my great love until now. I love you deeply and you set the bar very high for me. Dear companion, today I come to say goodbye to you so that you can rest in peace and so that I may have peace. I ask you to bless me so that I can find a love like you and take care of me until the end."

I ask her *Soul* how she feels, and she says very calm, very at peace. I then invite one more character, who walks forward, and she goes to look for him. She takes his hands while she looks at him tenderly.

"There is your new love. This new love is going to amuse you. And this one already buries you!!!"

How nice it is sometimes to close with laughter. How happy it makes us feel that, between tears and laughter, we are healing. I never get tired of the feeling it gives me to see the constellation dry tears while laughing. Feeling that repair and relief in others is what feeds the strength of my soul that drives me to continue walking this path.

Let's share the learning: What is not elaborated is repeated

When we repeat stories, it is because some story is not closed. In matters of love, it may be because I was left with some anger and in a certain way the energy stagnates. When this happens and by being trapped in that moment or time, I attract similar people and situations to complete this learning. The constellation can help you shorten the time and with a farewell, a cry or a hug you close what needed to be closed. Only then will a new stage open for your life since something new does not appear until the previous one is concluded. This is valid for companies, businesses, relationships with bosses, employees, friends, etc.

Constellation: Woman (Septennium # 9 - Age 56 to 63), entrepreneur

Topic: Little communication with the eldest daughter and concern for the family and children

"Dear. What brings you here? How many children do you have?"

"Four."

"Ages?"

"36, 34, 31 and 28. And my subject is my eldest daughter. She has a hard time communicating."

"Like your husband."

"Yes, like my husband. You have to get things out of her with a corkscrew. And she had violence problems with a boyfriend. She is separated with two children and then she got married to this boy. I didn't know him, but her ex-girlfriend came to tell us that our daughter was dating a guy who wasn't a good person. We talked to her, but she got angry with us. She has a very good bond with her siblings, but not with us. Luckily, she eventually stopped dating that guy, but I know that later she had an episode of violence. We found out because she asked someone else to tell us. Now everything is calm, the guy didn't appear again. But the issue is how do I get to it from my place. How do I let her know, even though she knows, that my intention is good, I don't want to tell her who she has to go out with."

"And you told her?"

"Yes, but she is very difficult."

"Send her a message, an email, well thought out, carefully, reread it a couple of times, let it mature for a day and read it again. It is a delicate message. Like you did with your husband."

She remains silent for a few moments during which she leans her head forward. Immediately she places her head high, takes a deep breath and continues.

"The other issue is my son. I do have a lot of dialogue with him, but I don't think I know how to do what I should do to help him."

"What would that be like?" I ask her with genuine curiosity.

"And how to maintain him," she continues without listening.

"Take care of him financially, do you mean?"

"Yes, but we told him no."

"And then?"

"All good. He didn't ask us, or he did, but he told us not to give it to him."

I lean my body forward and look at her with confusion, then ask her for help.

"I wouldn't be understanding."

"It's like he asked us for a loan it and he was going to give it back to us, but my husband said no. He's 31 years old. I need him to become independent and grow. It's his problem."

"Well, yes. But what is your fear?"

"That I have two relatives who died at the age of 30."

"But he's 31! It's already happened. And most importantly, life and death are not in our hands."

In a thick silence we began to work, and I told her:

"Let's constellate, but don't let the reason be fear of him dying. When you have your grandchildren and they turn 29, you are going to call me to see if I am alive to constellate them!!"

The heaviness of the atmosphere collapsed before the inevitable laughter; it was like refreshing rain on a summer day. But I don't want her to disconnect, so I ask her:

"Do you suspect that he is up to something strange?"

"No, I don't suspect anything of that."

"And how is your husband regarding this son?"

"Barbarous because he constellated."

"Oh great. Then trust the constellator!"

"Well, but I didn't tell you that I was the constellator!"

Despite the general laughter I got worried.

"Dear, I know you love constellating, but you have to be careful with constellating within the system to which you belong. Above all, when on top of that you are afraid for your children."

"Yes, of course, I might constellate it with a professional constellator."

"Well, let's constellate here then. What are we going to constellate about?"

"About my children, if I am standing where I have to be and so are they."

Let's go then. I ask her to choose her representative, her husband's representative, and the representatives of her four children, and I send them to do what they want and position themselves however they want.

Her *soul* is very attentive to the children. So, I ask her to observe:

"Look at it from the outside. It's as if your children are a flock of sheep and you two are the dogs that herd the sheep."

I ask the Representatives how they feel.

The oldest says he feels fine, he is looking at the siblings. The second says he doesn't feel anything. The third says he is uncomfortable in that place. The youngest says that everything is fine. The father says that he feels his wife is distant from him, as if lost.

And her *Soul* says she needs to look at them all the time, she needs to be there. And as she spoke, everyone ran away from her. The siblings got together and embraced each other. The oldest tells the mother that he needs her to stop staring at him and bothering him.

I ask them all to repeat and say in chorus:

"Dear mom, we love you and dad too. And it would be very good for everyone if you went on a trip, and for you to take care of dad who needs you more every day."

The R *Husband* walks towards her *Soul* and takes her in his arms. Seeing her calmer now, I ask her:

"What would you tell your children?

"That I love them. And the deep love and admiration I feel for them doesn't let me stop seeing them. And our children united is the best we can have."

The R *Father* remains silent but calm. Once again, I ask her *Soul* to tell her children:

"Dear children, go play and be happy because mom and dad love you, take care of you and protect you."

I ask the children to turn facing the future, with their parents behind them supporting them.

"How do you feel?" I ask everyone.

"Better," the children respond.

"Dad?"

"Very good."

"And the mother?"

"Ah… with a full heart."

Now I invite the *Consultant* to enter and embrace her *Soul*. The *Consultant* cries with joy, but she still asks:

"Do you think I'm doing right?"

I am a very educated man and I know that you should not answer a question with another question, but I couldn't contain myself. I looked at her and said:

"What do you think?"

She turned on her heels with a big smile, her face still streaked with tears, and sat up tall and proud.

Let's share the learning: Parental concern acts as crutches for children

How difficult it is for us to let go of our children to the point that there are parents that desperately need to pay attention to their lives and their health. There are times when this concern acts as crutches for them, where they feel the need to consult their parents' opinions regarding each decision. If as parents we access this information, perhaps it is good to focus on our lives and projects. In this way we would give our children a little air so that they can practice and make mistakes with their own decisions, which will be part of their own life learning.

This is also very valid for school-age children, especially during exam time. The parents' concern that he will not pass the exam weakens the child, since this feeling of control with distrust is perceived by the child as a lack of confidence, losing and giving up his own power (by not being able to make his commitment, he does not take care of their responsibilities either).

Constellation: Man (Septennium # 6 - Age 28 to 35), businessman

Topic: My wife 's son

"I want to constellate the issue of my wife's son and…. but I need her not to be present," he says as he looks at her with eyes that beg for mercy. She calmly gets up and walks towards the door.

"Perfect" I support the position but at the same time I warn "But dear, don't eat the whole pizza!"

I want to clarify that humor is part of who I am, it is part of my daily life in all areas of my life. It is one of my favorite tools that allows me to heal. And whenever I share it naturally, I can feel that it helps heal others as well. I live daily with difficult topics that come to my consultation, and thanks to humor, everyone leaves very well, strengthened and empowered.

We continue.

"My wife's son is seven years old, and I met her when the baby was one and a half years old. I never got involved in raising him because I believed it wasn't my place. Many times, we have conflicts between us and with him because of the way I treated him. And sometimes I think it's true that I haven't always treated him well."

"And today?"

"Today I also think I don't treat him well sometimes. And I think it's because of the anger I have with his father. Because he mistreated her long before, even when she was pregnant with my daughter. One time I got fed up and told him I was going to beat him to death. Before, the person affected by that bad relationship they had was their son. But when she was already pregnant with my daughter, I exploded. And the baby experiences all of this and perceives it. It is difficult for me to accept and forgive her ex-partner. I could never."

"Okay. Choose someone to represent you, someone to represent your wife, and someone to represent her ex-partner."

The chosen ones stood up and stand in the center of the room, and his *Soul* stood away from both of them, evidently in conflict and at odds.

I ask the representatives how they feel.

"I find it difficult to express myself," the *Soul* quickly responds, "I feel hard, and there is something in the way she looks at me that I feel diminishes me, or that she asks me for something with her gaze that seems easy or seems easy to her but *that* I cannot do."

"I feel good, I don't need you to express yourself," says *R Wife*. The soul begins to respond in a low voice.

"I don't know what I feel. I don't know if it's fear."

Turning towards the *Consultant* I say:

"Look at your posture, you are the same as that of your *Soul*, shoulders slumped, diminished, de-energized."

"I feel like he can, I trust him, but I feel like he doesn't trust himself," *R Wife* adds.

I intervene, again addressing the *Consultant*:

"I think that anyone, if you don't feel up to it, is going to make you feel bad. Not just his ex."

His *Soul* moves away from her and says he feels more relieved walking away.

"And obviously, if you move away, you see her smaller, but… you're further away!" I intervene and incorporate several new representatives. "His mother and a long line of male ancestors, because this man needs to graduate himself as a man."

"Look at your father, grandfather, great-grandfather, great-great-grandfather, great-great-great-grandfather… Everyone looking at you," I say, pointing to the row and inviting him to look at them, to see them, to feel them. And I continue:

"Where did your ancestors come from?"

"Of Italy, of the war," I hear him say in a soft tone, as if delivered, and I point to those men again.

"They survived the wars and came to tell you that you have everything you need to have a great woman, to be able to look her in the eyes and be able to tell her that you love her."

First, I ask his *Soul* to lean on the long line of his male ancestors. And then I ask the *Consultant* to enter the field and take the place of his *Soul,* which is his place. I ask him to lean on all those men who are there so that he can lean on them and that in their name he can carry forward his happiness.

He leans and encourages himself to let go, to surrender. There he remains rocking for a few long seconds.

"How do you feel?" I inquire.

"Good, calm, energetic, strong," he replies, although his voice certainly did not reveal that strength. But it is also true that the long and intense hours we have been working have us all very exhausted.

The *Consultant* now walks towards *his* R *Wife* who is waiting for him with a smile, and they hug and he whispers I love you to her.

I ask him how he feels, to which he responds that he feels fine but that he has almost no voice. He says with great vocal effort that he feels bigger.

"You're bigger," I correct him.

The R *Wife* spontaneously tells him that together they will be able to. I intervene and ask *his* R *Woman* to look at him, take his hands and say: "I accept you; I choose you and I love you with everything you have."

We all felt a lump in our throats when we saw them melt into a hug of pure dedication. He says that he is exhausted, that his fears have exhausted him.

I ask her how she feels, and she says she feels like a fire in her body.

I now incorporate a representative for her son, who enters the field enraged and begins to yell at them:

"You are rubbish, everything is rubbish, you are the worst, what you say is #$#"$#," everyone go to the #$"$#"$%"!!!!!"

I intervene again and incorporate the representative of their daughter who is standing next to her parents, and the *Consultant* continues in his attempt to explain to the boy that he is there to love him and educate him, but the boy asks to speak, interrupting him and says in a loud voice supplicant:

"I need you to tell me something from the heart."

The *Consultant* approaches him with the little energy he has left, stops in front of the child and, already sunk in immense desolation and guilt, hugs him and begs him to forgive him for everything that made him suffer.

I leave him for a few minutes to recover and then I ask him to stand in front of the R *of his wife's ex* (the child's father) and say these words to him:

"I recognize you as my wife's previous partner and as the father of this child. I am very angry. I am very angry with your attitude because you put the lives of my wife and daughter at risk. I ask you to put yourself in your place and take care of your son as true men do."

I ask the son how he feels, and he says that it bothers him that the mother does not approach him (he remains next to his sister). "It's okay for others to approach me, but she doesn't do anything. Like she lives in a cloud of illusions. I see the three of them happy, they look like a McDonald's box."

Now it is the R *Father of the Child* who I ask how he feels who answers:

"I'm doing my best; my life really is chaos."

"The child approaches the father because he needs his father. The child is going to need to process it, it is difficult. He discovered that his father leaves his mother pregnant and that he has a brother on his father's side who is 10 months younger than him, he lives in a family that he does not feel is his, and he has a father who is not fulfilling his role. Here, on the one hand, a lot of patience is needed on your side and the child must be given time and professional help."

The *Consultant* is silent, exhausted, barely there, and shuffles back to his chair.

"In conclusion, you have to stay big, not smaller, diminished. She needs a man who can give her security and support."

Let's share the learning: The importance for a man of taking the ancestral masculine strength

It is very important that every man takes the strength of his male Ancestral line, to transform into a man, find his place, be able to establish limits and take charge without fear of what belongs to him. In this constellation we were able to witness the growth and strength that the *Consultant* achieved and thanks to this he will be able to be in harmony with his partner and the blended family they have.

This is also totally valid for women who need to tap into the Ancestral Feminine energy that resides behind their own biological mother.

Constellation: Woman (Septennium # 7 - Age 42 to 49), businesswoman

Topic: Hypertension

"In 2015 I was diagnosed with hypertension. The doctor now told me that it is emotional, so he took me off the medication. And from that moment on, my blood pressure shot up several times."

"What happened in 2015 that triggered the issue of pressure?"

"A couple and work issue because we worked together."

"Did you close the subject of him?"

"He ran away leaving a pile of debts, and then he did it again, but I don't think that's the issue there."

"Well let's see. Choose someone to be your *Soul* and someone else."

They both enter the field and immediately her *Soul* moves away from the R *Unknown* because it gave her chills. She was shaking. I bring in the R *of the Fugitive* and her *Soul* says that her arrival calmed her, but she doesn't want to look at him. She is very angry.

She said that she was with him for nine years and he was the one who handled all the business. I ask her to address these words to the R *of the Fugitive*:

"It hurt me a lot that our dreams were not fulfilled, but I thank you for accepting my daughter. Thank you for loving my daughter, for having been a father to her. I was disillusioned by your ambition, and it melted me. To this day I receive letters looking for you and demanding money that forces me to go out and explain that I have nothing to do with it. It's a small town and my image is at stake. I loved you deeply and you broke my heart."

The R *of the Fugitive* kneels in front of her soul, but she says that she is still very angry with him, even though he asks for forgiveness. His shoulders are heavy. He doesn't want him to look at her anymore.

"Would you tell him something else?"

"That he let me down, and that I'm taking charge of things that don't belong to me."

I ask her to add:

"And from now on I release myself and I release you with love so that we can be happy. Thank you."

I ask her *Soul* how she feels, and she says she feels calm.

And that is. That was the origin. And once the source is found, it is unlocked.

While all this was happening, the R *Unknown*, which represented hypertension, moved away and sat down, disappearing from the Constellation.

Let's share the learning: Our restorative Soul

We cannot return to the past, but with this tool that is the Constellation, which is worked with the soul, we can from within relive the event that caused the trauma, return to the right moment, repair it and return to the present. If that specific issue that was constellated was the original cause, at the end of it, that situation ends and is disarmed. But sometimes that is not the origin, but rather that situation is a replica of a previous event.

For example, in cases of suicide: suicide may have been established in the suicide from a previous ancestral instance and he may not have been the first. Perhaps the first was six generations ago.

For this it is very important to be attentive to listening and very accurate in the diagnosis before starting the Constellation. It is very important to have a good understanding of the situation and context of the person who Constellates.

Constellation: Woman (Septennium # 6 - Age 28 to 35) Yoga teacher

Topic: I am a lover

"What brings you here?"

"Well, I had thought before…"

"No, not before. Now."

"Well... it's my hidden relationship thing... and I committed to making it hidden," she explains nervously and laughs. She continues:

"I don't want to be in that situation, but nevertheless... I'm back. And then I leave him… but I came back again."

"Did you ever tell him?"

"The few times we talk about it he seems comfortable."

"Obviously! How can he not be comfortable? You are a beautiful young woman in her thirties!!"

"And he is almost twenty years older."

"Ah well, he's obviously an opportunist."

"What happens is that when I leave him, I don't so it from the place I should, that is, I leave him because I know I should, but not because I want to."

A participant, who knows her, asks to speak, the *Consultant* allows her, and she tells her that her key is in her catchphrase of "being of service." I watch her laugh, and I tell her that yes, she was very brave in playing that role of good girl.

"I want him to choose me," she says with anguish in her voice.

"I don't want to be with another person. I'm faithful."

"Well. Okay. Choose someone to represent you and someone for Mr. X."

"I'm very naive. I'm not very romantic. But I'm naive."

I call two *R Unknowns* and ask them to position themselves wherever they want. Both are placed between them, who are facing each other and far away. *R Mr. X* says that one of the *R Unknown* bothers him and wants her to leave, that he tries to step away, but she doesn't let him, he can't stop looking at her. He says he is only interested in the *Consultant.* I call another *R Unknown* and now he says that, with the third participant, he is only interested in the new one. Again, I relocate them, now I place her *Soul* next to the new *R Unknown* and the *R of Mr. X* says that this duo attracts him a lot and the rest doesn't matter to him, however, he clarifies that when the new R looks at him it makes him very nervous, and his hands sweat. Coincidentally, the new representative is the commitment, the ring.

"You are blindly in love with him, and you cannot see another love, even if it is in front of you. You have to pressure him and see if he chooses you. If he goes out on a limb for you, great, otherwise it's better for him to stay away from you. Because you could be just someone new, he then gets tired of. And one day he can get tired, dazzle with someone else and leave, leaving you with a child. And you in the role of lover, the second.

The R of *Mr. X* shares that when he listened to me talk about the son his nerves were gone.

The *Consultant* is restless, it can be seen in her tense and hunched body posture, in her fearful smile and in her confused look.

"I don't dare tell him that. Because I don't think he's going to want to commit to me."

"How long do you think you can stay like this?"

"It's been four years."

I observe her, I see her, I tell her:

"You started before you were thirty, in a few more years you will be a critical age for a woman."

"Maybe he wants children and ends up having them with the other woman and doesn't dare to take the leap if he doesn't see that you want them. But you won't know unless you go all in. Continuing here, in this area of indefinitions and denials, can deprive you of being *a mother*. I ask you to please look at yourself and see yourself as I see you, as the people who love you and who are there for you and who do what they have to do to make you happy to see you. And then I ask you to see him. You know how much I appreciate you. So... I would tell you that the decision is in your hands."

Let's share the learning: Every lover is at the service of marriage.

The first time I heard this phrase, I had a hard time understanding it. If we understand a lover as something more than a person, we can extend it to work, a passion, a hobby or even an addiction.

I once treated a man of about 45 years old, who had been fired from his job eight months ago. His wife asked him to look for a job, since she was the one who was maintaining the house. But he had a great passion for electric trains, he had a model that covered a huge room with an impressive collection of trains. That hobby had transformed into his passionate lover, in which he wanted her wife to go to work to be with her. When he wasn't playing, he was thinking about her.

Like this case, there are many and these occur when both are NOT available. In this case, surely the woman has work as a lover, or another man, for that matter it is the same.

When someone comes to see me who no longer wants to be with their partner and, for example, wants to get divorced, the first thing I tell them is that, if they have a lover, they should leave them and focus on their partner to try to maintain the bond. Since when there are no lovers between the couple, they will be the only ones who have to face each other and whether or not to sustain the relationship.

Day three

The rest was deep and restorative for everyone. Specially after having gone to bed past midnight and having enjoyed a wonderful bonfire in which we sang and delivered burdens and sorrows to the fire. This last day dawned cold with a clear, blue sky. Without having left yet, we are already missing the place, but breakfast cheers us up and fills our body, mind and heart with joy.

We walked through the beautiful landscape towards our space, energized and eager to move forward and close. I share a few words with everyone and observe their bodies, their postures, their expressions in order to take the emotional temperature of each one and be able to put together the closing plan of the seminar for each participant. Everyone says they feel happy, at peace and light. Honestly... I don't know if you could ask for much more!

Constellation: Woman (Septennium #9 - Age 56 to 63) recently retired administrative employee

Topic: The relationship with my husband

"How are you dear? What would you like to Constellate on this occasion?"

"I want to Constellate my husband's relationship with me. We've been together for a long time, but he doesn't have a job and he's at home a lot."

"And yes, it is complicated to have a man at home all the time! You are a very active woman, your husband is somewhat withdrawn, perhaps a little depressed. You have to leave your house, and I tell you this because it is even therapeutic. This is a matter of life or death for you. You have a lot of energy; you need to do things all the time and now you are newly retired. Going from total activity to being at home with him for long periods of time is going to put you down badly."

"Yes, he is very closed, he never speaks. Well, almost never. But when he speaks, he explodes. It's very extreme. He listens to the radio at full volume. If I ask him to turn it down, he gets angry and turns it off. He watches a lot of football, those who argue among themselves and shout, and I am overwhelmed by his radio, his football, and also his silence."

"Buy him a headset!"

"Yes, maybe."

"Well, come on. Find someone for you and someone for him."

"I believe he is silent because he has a lot of internal conversations."

"Well yes, he talks to himself!"

"Don't you see? He who speaks alone has many conversations with the world, with his world."

I invite her to choose someone to represent her *Soul*, and someone to represent her husband.

As soon as she enters the field, her *Soul* begins to walk in a small circle, looking down and with her arms crossed, disconnected.

I ask her *Soul* how she feels, and she tells me that the soles of her feet feel cold, and that she feels restless.

"And yes, look what you are! A caged beast. I would tell you that, for his mental health, no, rather, for his physical health and your emotional health, change your focus to yourself."

"He is done already with his activities. Not you, you need other challenges, not just feeding the chickens. You force yourself to be in restless in a little square. Do you remember how your legs hurt? Look at you, walking without stopping."

Now I ask her how her R *Husband's* how he feels, and he answers:

"I don't understand the situation. I don't know why she walked away from me."

"The ray of light over there catches my attention, I imagine it is warm and makes me want to go there," says her *Soul*.

"Follow the impulse," I encourage her. At the same time, I add another character to the field, and ask:

"How do you feel with that other character there next to you?"

"I feel like she is blocking the light. I would move her."

"How do you feel about him, who is still silent?"

"It doesn't bother me."

"See? He follows you. You do what you want, he will follow you."

"I don't know. He is very structured, very closed. Imagine, he doesn't like when it's 5pm and we are not bathed."

We couldn't help it and we all burst out laughing. And she laughs too, with that innocent attitude.

"I'm serious!" she explains between laughs, "the other day he looked at the clock and said: Ohhh look it's 10 to 5 and we're not bathed!"

Laughter revives in the room like a shower of stars.

"What did he say with you were coming here? Did he ask you to coordinate your clocks?"

Some are already crying from laughter; she laughs more than anyone.

We all laughed at it, we had fun for a few minutes, but we didn't take away even a bit of seriousness from it.

I ask *R Husband* how he feels.

"I feel like someone is grabbing my arms, they move them, but it's not me."

"Let's add your children," I propose and continue investigating.

"How does R *Husband* feel now that the children are here?"

"Strange, on one hand, I felt more strength, but on the other hand I am kind of worried."

"He worries about his children," I tell the *Consultant.*

"What I see makes me distressed, I feel like they don't care about me and that they don't understand me, I feel bad," R *Husband* continues to tell us.

"The children can't stop looking over there, they're watching both of you. The boy looks at the father and the girl at the mother."

Her *Soul* says she doesn't feel observed at all, that she feels good, that she has fun.

But the R*'s of the Children* look back, they do not feel the freedom to look towards their futures. The boy approaches the father because he needs him and kneels in front of him.

Now I ask R *Daughter* how she feels, and she says she feels good, fun. She feels complicit with her mother.

I now incorporate another participant who represents life and place her behind everyone. The R *Daughter* has her back looking at the mother who is in a fit of laughter and moves towards life and then towards her daughter while she is looking for the rays of the sun. I see that the daughter is so dependent on her mother's approval that she cannot live her life and move toward her future.

I ask her *Soul* to stay in front of *her Daughter's R* and repeat these words to her: "My work is done, there is no more, now it's your turn," but she can't stop laughing. She is totally disconnected from her husband who is located in the background hugging their son.

I ask her *Soul* again to speak to her daughter and tell her: "I retired, and now it's your turn," and this time she does it.

The father advances towards the daughter, takes her decisively, and places her in front of her mother and next to her son, her brother. He now places his wife behind the children and finally he places himself behind the children, next to his wife.

I observe carefully and inform The *Consultant*:

"Life is waiting for you to make the decision and the rest will take care of itself. Your husband will be rustic, he is a country man, but he knows about life, births, weaning. Your husband knows about the cycles of life. He is one of those who would grab your son and tell him: "Son, there is no more milk, you need to go out and look for your food and your shelter. It's time for you to grow up. I'll give you six months of free rent, you either pay for the seventh or you leave, because this way I'm hurting you."

The father adds a few words to her and tells her that she is very important to him.

"Now, beyond this, you need to do something for yourself. He also wants to make changes, like tango class, and that already means the world to him and for you it is almost an irrelevant thing. You have to find what makes you happy and tell him that if he loves you, he has to support you because if he doesn't, he's going to bury you, because you're going to die locked up there."

I ask R *Husband* how he feels.

"I don't feel like I don't want her to do her things, what happens to me is that I need her to look at me, to really look at me."

"I recommend that you read my book "*Etapas Vitales*" or search the Internet for the topic of The Septennium and look at which septennium he is going through. Because what fears correspond to your Septennium is important. If you don't help him with those fears, he's going to get worse. You have to reinforce that you love him, and because you love him you need to do other things. But trust. He loves you very much and he is very proud of his family. He's a very good guy."

Let's share learning: The Good and the Bad Conscience

The person who discovered these concepts, which he defined as good and bad conscience, was Bert Hellinger at the time he was a priest. What caught his attention was that when people went to the confessional, they considered their "faults or sins" in a very different way. Until he discovered that it was related to values, loyalties and family models.

Saying that one is passing through Spaces of Good Consciousness means that what I am doing is well seen by my family, my parents, which would be group consciousness. It is feeling in a state of tranquility, acceptance and inclusion, it is feeling like you belong to the family. Since one of the greatest fears is exclusion. For example, following the career that our parents want, staying married, even if we are unhappy, continuing with the parents' business, even if the vocation is different, etc. You will surely have some examples of your own to contribute to the list!

Saying that one is passing through Spaces of Bad Consciousness means being or doing what one wants to be or do, even if the family does not welcome this.

The risk one runs when traveling through these spaces is that of exclusion, since our belonging is at stake. Example, choosing the love that is not blessed by parents, not continuing with traditions, etc.

We spend much of our lives alternating from one space to another. While in a space of good conscience we feel the tranquility of belonging, in that of bad conscience, it provides us with learning that allows us to grow. The only place we can belong and grow at the same time is in the womb. Once we go out into the world, everything changes, and this wheel of consciousness begins to rotate and alternate.

Constellation: Woman (Septennium # 6 - Age 28 to 35), senior master builder, entrepreneur

Topic: Launching your own family project.

"That topic you were talking about, the Spaces of bad conscience and good conscience ordered what I want to constellate. I realized that I am a bad conscience... in full form!!! I feel this way with my in-laws and making me feel like I have a bad conscience pushes my husband away, pushes away the projects we have together; I want to send them all away to #$## and grab him and take him away and do our thing. But I know the cost is very high. I feel that what I want to do is good, but I don't know if he follows me in this position."

"But there is a time for everything. Sometimes in six months a window of opportunity can close."

"Yes, but we are on time. But I know what you say about time is true because I already feel like I'm getting angry. How can you believe that I handle it? I feel guilty. They want me to be a housewife and I want to be a businesswoman. And that's why they see me as arrogant and not as if we can simply want something else. He can make his own decisions and I need him to make them."

"I think the time has come for you to talk less and for him to talk more to the outside world. He has to talk more to defend himself or to generate the dynamic you need to implement what you want as a family project."

"This year I didn't do anything for my birthday, because I didn't feel like it. But my father-in-law did not greet me. And that hurt me."

"Did you tell him?"

"No, because I feel like every time I speak it's a bomb."

"When they see their son taking care of the kids and I'm locked up studying, they get outraged."

"Well. Let's get to work then. I want you to choose someone for you, that is, your *Soul* and someone for your husband, two representatives for your mother and father, and two more representatives for your father-in-law and your mother-in-law."

As she chooses them, they enter the field and I ask them to do what they want, to move, and to find a place for themselves. And so, they do it. When I observe, the picture of the situation is very clear. I explain it.

"You both are in the eyes of everyone from both families. Notice how this formation is a continuation of the exercise you did at the beginning."

The mother breathes on his neck. The father has him in front of him, close and feels proud, but that close distance is very emasculating.

We see how at the moment the two of them hug, the environment begins to fade away. He feels more relieved than when he came in, when he was complaining that his neck pain.

Her father and mother are proud of their daughter. Her *Soul* would want *her Husband's R Father* to look at her, but he doesn't look at her. She says that she doesn't feel anything bad, but she would like to be seen, taken into account for business.

I ask them to look forward, to which her *Soul* responds.

"I'm already far away, in the trees over there. This is going a little slow for me!" Laughter from everyone, especially from the *Consultant*.

When they took two steps forward, they caused the four fathers to line up behind the two of them.

I ask them to remember what we talked about the space of good conscience and bad conscience. Those two steps of bad conscience are the ones they have to go through. You, I say, addressing her *Soul*, are the driving force and he, and I point this out to her husband, are her support, the back.

The *Husband's R Father* says he feels he needs to push them forward.

"Yes, but only now," says her *Soul* in a defiant tone. She is silent for a few seconds, and she leans against her parents who are holding her behind her, she stays for a few minutes, then she rejoins and makes an acclamation.

"That felt so nice! When I was able to lean on my parents, I was able to stop looking so far ahead and I wanted to be more in the "here and now," not so far ahead."

"You need to be well united while traveling through shifting lands, which are the most difficult, and you can miss this unique opportunity. If you don't do it, in ten years he may still be working with his father, and she may be making her life with someone else."

"But how do I confront them?" he asks, half stunned and exhausted.

"You just don't have to face them. Focus on the horizon, not on the sides, as if this were a race. You can't look at the person next to you or behind you because you lose. You always run looking forward. You first have to agree and understand your project and business one hundred percent. And you have to be together, united, without fissures, without distractions, dedicated to each other in complete trust."

I look at her *Soul* and tell her:

"If you get involved with your mother-in-law you lost. Focus on what's important. Notice how the environment cleared and everything lined up behind you when you joined. If you enter without being ONE, your own systems absorb you, take you back and your project falls. Therefore, I believe that your way out involves keeping your project, your venture, a secret until it starts to work. This is the secret, the union. The important thing is the first fifty meters."

"How cool," *the Consultant* complains jokingly, "I have to do the first fifty meters!"

"Yes, you have to do them," I answer, and thank joke with him "But then he supports you, you and the others."

"You have to start with a specific plan, make the forms, set dates, everything, get it started and that's it."

Let's share learning: The cost of our dreams

In this constellation something happened that often happens and that is a project or undertaking that a person or couple wants to carry out. Outside of the jokes that arose, both come from two very different family systems and realities and in their own way are traveling through spaces of good conscience. He is working in a family business, being part of his family's plan to continue it, and she, an innate entrepreneur with leadership skills. The challenge is to be able to come together to realize their desires and start a business. This will cause Him to need to go through a space of insights and be the owner of his destiny. Those are the fifty meters in which She is going to have to support him and perhaps hold him up.

Here we can also see how a constellation in the work or organizational field provides an action plan to get out of the current situation and look to the future.

It's time for a break.

Our minds and our souls demand it from us. We went out to lunch, to stretch for a while and recharge our batteries on this beautiful sunny day that invites us to enjoy.

Now renewed, we went back to work. As a colorful note of the day, a participant delighted us with a stand-up style monologue that lifted us up into the air with laughter, succumbed us to the depths with her tears and finally gave us a loving and hopeful horizon to look towards.

*Let's share the learning: **When do we know we have found true love?***

When we get ready to start, an interesting topic emerges from the conversation.

When do we know that we have found the true love of our lives?

The question ends up in my lap and I feel all eyes waiting for an opinion for which I stop and think for a few moments. I believe that only on our deathbed will we know who it was. We need every possible distance and perspective to answer that question. Because sometimes we choose well from the project, for example, becoming a *mother*, starting a family, breaking with family dynamics, fulfilling ourselves in our professional career, or any project, but I don't know if we really choose from love. How much is love and not some fear that causes a certain illusion and makes us believe that it is love?

Also, I think asking ourselves that question puts love outside. And love is within one. When you have a loving relationship with yourself you can find someone with whom to share that love you already have. Otherwise, it is searching from emptiness. When we start to work on ourselves and on our emptiness, we find ourselves and only then can we see the other and see where we chose them from.

Constellation: Woman (Seventh # 10 - Age 63 to 70), holistic therapist

Topic: Finish her house, to have your workplace

"What do you want to constellate?"

"Why the house is not moving forward, my house, our house, my husband's and mine. And that of my children."

"No, it's not of your children."

"They are going to inherit it when I die."

"Yes, but until that day it is not theirs."

"True," she says and thinks for a few moments. She immediately returns and explains:

"The issue is that we do not advance, we take out a loan, it advances a little, but then it ends. And I tell my husband to paint something, and he doesn't do it. And when I ask him why he doesn't do it if he used to do it for others, he tells me that this is his house, and he is going to do it whenever he wants. And he continues with the loans, but I don't just need money, I need him to put a nail, change the leather on the shins and he doesn't do it. All the money goes to the car that we took from 0 KM that has been in the workshop for a long time and takes all the money. I want to know what's happening, why don't we move forward. I need to finish that house to have my space to work."

"Well, let's get to work then," I order her jokingly and ask her to put together her plot.

"I chose one to represent you and another for your husband, I ask and invite the R *of your Space* that you need to work on to also join. Then I also invite the credits." The representatives stand alone on the field. I see that her *Soul* is very angry.

And I see the husband, stunned by the R's *of the Credits* that hover around him and make him tense.

"Look at your husband. He is very worried about the credits, and you are worried about the house. You are worried about your space that is not materialized."

I ask R *Husband* how he feels, and he says that he feels that the loans help him, and he is right, they help him, but they also cause him worry and anguish because he is in debt.

Now I invite the jobs that may come his way.

"You went to concentrate on your activities so as not to depend on him. So don't depend on him. Focus on your work. That will create space. And then you will do your work in your space. Look, his work is not going to work out, look at the work, he is dizzy. With his level of stress, it's going to be difficult. Observe how the field is divided into him and his concerns on one side and you with your concerns on the other," I mark the clear division that is a striking crack.

"How much money do you need to finish it?"

"I don't know," she answers agitated.

"Ask for the budget and tell him that now you are going to do it on your own and you are going to hire the people yourself and you are going to manage the credits. Like you always did. You maintain the house, do you remember? Once that is done, you will be able to help him from another side. He can't help you in this. Get into that circle that was formed on your side of the crack, let yourself be hugged by it and kiss your husband and say to yourself "I'm going to be able to."

"Now you will be able to return to your own thing, this move and having been in your own home for the first time paralyzed you. You needed all this time to sort yourself out, to realize that it wasn't a dream. Everything that happened was to wake you up from sleep. You are already awake and one step away from being able to literally close your space, since the walls are in half, only the openings and the ceiling are missing. Take care of organizing your house and your husband. Be yourself again. You can!"

Sharing learning: The importance of our place

How many of us have our place, our space, from a workshop with tools, our desk, our office, our corner. Without it is like we lack our place in the world. I travel a lot doing this wonderful job, but in each city, I have my place, my corner, that little smell that makes you feel at home. What is your place in the world? Do you have a place? If you don't have it, look for it or make it!

We have all constellated. The countryside is at peace. And we are all looking forward to a break for some well-paid effort, relaxing, and going for a walk. The still radiant sun shines on the placid lake while the air caresses everything. Before we disperse, I ask everyone to find a place that inspires them and to write something, whatever they want to share with you, the readers, about this experience they have had.

Incredibly, we had a little bit of time left over and everyone wanted to continue working! How can it be? Aren't you exhausted and sick of listening to me? It seems not... I admire their energy and their tireless work to lead the life they want to lead.

We then take advantage of this surge of renewed energy and prepare to do one last systemic dynamic that we could call "Honoring our vital stages."

Exercise 5: Systemic dynamics "Honoring our vital stages"

Instruction:

Although the ideal exercise would be to form groups and have as many members as there are life stages grouped by seven years, I have adapted it to the number of attendees.

Then we put together groups of 6 people where each one will represent a stage of life, divided into 10-year stages ranging from childhood, adolescence, adulthood and old age.

They position themselves in front of each stage and do what they need, they hug her, they say goodbye, they revere her, they cry... whatever they need to make peace with them.

Closing and Farewell

This seminar has been a spectacular experience. Not only the weather, the place, the food, everything beyond our expectations but, and mainly, because of the human group that attended. And the weather, the place and the food have been dreamlike. But like everything, the end came. Although we still have a snack left!

I'm just going to add a few words.

I sincerely hope that this seminar has been useful to the participants and also to the readers. I long from the bottom of my soul that we can move forward every day towards our dreams.

Today I am fulfilling two dreams. The first is to carry out this seminar here and accompany you in your processes. There comes a time when the teachers leave, and they are no longer there, without being a teacher I encourage myself to help people with my tools. Because that is my vocation: to feel useful and that you are better, resolving and being.

And the other is to finish my first book dedicated especially to Constellations from what are my Intensive Seminars, which would be my 15th. Also, to begin to tell a little of my personal story and experiences so that they can be left to my children and grandchildren. Unfortunately, I was not able to tell the story of my previous ones, except for the luck I had in being able to enjoy them and I feel very happy to be able to honor them in these lines with my memory and love.

Both dreams would have been impossible to achieve without you.

That is why I thank each of you because you are the ones who give meaning to my work and my life.

With a great applause we close this seminar, and we launch into the race shouting… Let's have a snack!!!!

Testimonials

I leave with a full, happy and empowered soul to start working on the (woman) I want to be tomorrow. They were three days of intense work of looking inward, of working and getting rid of fears, anxieties, backpacks and much more. I thank each of my cohabitation partners, since thanks to them I was able to lift the veil of many things that I was not prepared to see or work on.

A huge thank to Claudio who, with his warmth and talent as a facilitator, allows me to advance one step further on this wonderful path of the constellations in order to get closer to the being I want to be.

I hope that each and every one of us can take a small step forward on this path called life. I hope we see each other again very soon with new challenges to overcome.

Thank you for allowing me to collaborate and trusting me as a participant. I take away a lot of information from each constellation.

Things that resonated strongly in my head and soul:

1. *That one chooses one's destiny or ends up being part of someone else's plan.*
2. *Role of parents to challenge our children to make them stronger and fighters.*

> 3.　　Write my short, medium or long-term goals, such as: putting myself first, starting with accepting and loving myself. Stop taking care of everyone out of the need to please and be accepted.
>
> Here's to many more shared encounters... I say see you soon with great affection.

> In this search for being, I rediscovered the warrior in me, and I was able to visualize my family system, say goodbye to my father, accept my mother and my sister with love and thank every single thing that happened to me that made me stronger.
>
> I came restless, with uncertainty and I am leaving calmer, looking towards the future with more clarity regarding what I want and what I am going to do to be.

> Nine of us who traveled from Concepción del Uruguay arrived in the town of Capilla del Señor. We found a wonderful paradisiacal place full of nature, large trees, diverse birds, a lake, an extensive meadow and autumn coloring the landscape.
>
> I arrived very happy to have been allowed to come, to want to be here and to have been able to be here. When the whole group arrived, we introduced ourselves and Claudio, humble and friendly, greeted us and invited us to have a snack and then meet in the living room to start the activities.
>
> After introducing ourselves, he asked us what topics we were coming to work on or see. I really wasn't clear about what had brought me up or maybe I was scared to touch on the topic that

bothers me the most in my life, since it is my big secret, and I didn't know if I wanted to say it. Maybe for fear of knowing and losing that love or for fear of being judged. Luckily, I was not the first to speak and as the other participants shared their topics, I became clearer.

It's like a kind of confessional, deciding the topic, becoming aware, recognizing where you are, your pain, your thoughts, your emotions.

Your shame goes away, you tell it, you lose the fear of being judged, and you free yourself, you accept yourself, just as you are at this moment. And you take charge, responsible for your decisions and open the door to change, to walk towards the life you dream of.

After almost three days together, of seeing and participating in eighteen Constellations, of sharing empowerment dynamics, of organizing priorities, of changing life paradigms towards the confidence that I can have and do what makes me happy, I am leaving with the strength to act towards achieving my desires, to risk what I want, without fear of what people will say, with the strength and support of my family and with the necessary information to make decisions for growth, to be more myself, free and naïve in love.

I thank Claudio for this meeting, for offering himself so openly and sharing his experience and knowledge.

I thank the place, the nature that contained us, the wonderful people who took care of us, and the warmth of the group that allowed me to learn more and heal.

It is my first constellation and it has been very strong for me since I have realized how much pain the death of my son has caused me more than twenty years ago and that I have not yet healed.

I came with expectations of what I would be, since I considered that I did not know myself and I leave knowing what I have to repair and where I am located. I have sensations, emotions, sadness and joy in my body. Because I feel like I am embarking on my path, not only to heal but to be who I want to be and not how I have been limited to.

I came here with some expectations, not very clear, of healing a chronic health problem. The doctors I consulted did not give me any answers or effective treatment. I was also not sure how to approach the problem at hand.

After witnessing some Constellations of other people, I decided to constellate my family: father, mother, and I have been able to understand things about my family past, about my ancestors that I was really unaware of. I took away a very important experience, and the expectation of having cured my health problem.

They were three intense and incredible days. I came with low expectations without knowing exactly what topic to constellate, I think it was the right decision to constellate my partner's son, that brought me tranquility and peace.

Being able to help others to a greater or lesser extent allowed me to understand that camaraderie, unity and, above all, mutual support, is what we need as a society to overcome any obstacle.

Constellate is Mother and Father.

Water source.

"Traveler in life."

"Knowledge is like water"

Thanks Angeles. Thank you, Claudio. Thank you to each of you.

I hug them.

I am grateful for the meeting place that has sustained us so wonderfully. Three days to return to the essentials, in the company of people also interested in healing, reconnecting and moving forward from peace. This experience has allowed me to see life from a purer and more genuine place. Accept what it is to embrace pain and thus transform it. Help others in their process. I found a vital meaning that I was not aware of, managing to tie up loose ends of my life, reaching a deeper awareness of myself and my story. Seeing is liberation, ordering oneself in one's system is love and accepting allows us to move forward and moving forward is living, because life always makes its way. Thanks to everything that made this coexistence possible. In others their stories, their looks, their shortcomings and beauties. I recognize myself and feel united to life to move forward.

Being born again is possible when we connect with love and accept what is. And so, the loom of life is continually woven. I learned about the necessary balance between the different areas of our lives, that many times go beyond our hypotheses, that love always seeks to reach, that what is rejected is repeated and that pain must be kneaded with a lot of compassion and truth. You can always be better; you have to persevere with good intentions.

Returning to order is returning to life, which always asks us to recognize ourselves, to transform by accepting our pains and our joys, to truly decide to live life to the fullest. I found a wonderful space to recognize and accept everything I bring and am, to return to the simple and the beauty and strength of sharing with others because we are not alone.

Thanks to the group, to Claudio, to the constellations, to the people of the reserve, the delicious food and the beautiful nature.

Thanks to life.

I came happy. I'm going expanded! It is always revealing to me what "comes out," what I "see" in this beautiful tool. Not only when you have traveled your own constellation but when you are chosen to participate in that of others.

Grateful for each role, a story in which I had to participate. I healed a lot. Beautiful group! And Claudio, with great seriousness and professionalism, ensures that in painful topics there is LIGHTNESS, LIGHT and HUMOR!!!

I highly recommend it. It is an RX of the soul that must be gone through.

This weekend of coexistence continues to open the way for me to the life that I decided to live a few years ago. In a few months I will turn sixty and the constellations have been the perfect tool to capitalize on what I have experienced, take in what is beautiful, strengthen myself, recognize myself as I am, let go with love of what did not do me good and understand that if we connect deeply with ourselves, we can do of the life we live a fantastic experience.

Like I always say!!!! This is magic... PURE MAGIC. We encounter our experiences, we move, we forgive, we understand, we accept, and we move forward...

Without burdens, without backpacks, without taking what does not belong and taking what we need... LOVE AND STRENGTH.

For several years now I have been walking in different places...

For a little over two years now (I have been walking) on this path that has no turning back (I usually call it the path of life), full of people willing to make a great change, full of courage to face and face oneself...

Willing to be happy.

Thank you for every experience, for every contribution and for the confidence in themselves, for just being able to be.

I have never felt so identified when I participated in a group constellation. At that moment I realized that I can be of service to others, as long as I feel like it. That I should say NO to satisfy my self-esteem as many times as I want.

Three-day coexistence, they told me, in a super quiet place, you are going to experience something different, and I didn't think about anything other than participating.

And here I am happy, fulfilled, we constellate, we get excited, we laugh like crazy, we share, and at the same time I leave renewed with one less backpack, because that is constellation, taking weight off your back, old pains that were previously solved with pills, not now, everything flows, thank you, Claudio Alberto González, thank you, God, for having crossed my path. Now I know what it is to forgive from the heart, to let go, to love without further ado.

Thank you, universe, for this wonderful place called La Reserva that sheltered us in the middle of nature.

I arrived at a spectacular place, where everything was a perfect combination.

The space, the people, the energies, everything at the service of family constellations. The soul movement was intense and healing. I feel happy to have participated and grateful both to my colleagues for what I experienced and to the constellator for the care and respect with which he handled each case.

Thank you all.

I came full of fear; tired of all the situation and conflict in my life... Everything I have I half enjoy, and I don't deserve that...

I leave strengthened in myself, knowing that the decisions I make from now on will only be for my well-being and not for others. And if I don't value myself, no one else will. Now I will be visible to everyone.

Epilogue

I have a whirlwind of thoughts in my head at the end of my third review of this book, yesterday I wrote six thousand words of a third book that I want to publish, I am awakening many actions within me. I am happy to write a section called "My Notes," it will help me in future editions.

My editors advise me to write and do, they repeat to me that the path is shown when you walk it.

I am very happy and proud of how the book is turning out! I will take advantage of printing it in Spain and it is no small thing since it is the land of my ancestors!

Until next time! Dear reader, you're counting on me!

If you have made it this far, I promise to accompany you forever!

Contents

What is a Systemic Dynamics exercise and what is it for?

Opposites come together 83